P9-CJM-111

WITHDRAWN

Haiti

Haiti

BY NEL YOMTOV

Enchantment of the World™
Second Series

Children's Press®

An Imprint of Scholastic Inc.

NEW YORK   TORONTO   LONDON   AUCKLAND   SYDNEY
MEXICO CITY   NEW DELHI   HONG KONG
DANBURY, CONNECTICUT

Frontispiece: A fishing boat and net on the beach at Saint-Marc

Consultant: John Garrigus, Associate Professor, Department of History, University of Texas at Arlington

Please note: All statistics are as up-to-date as possible at the time of publication.

Book production by The Design Lab

Library of Congress Cataloging-in-Publication Data
Yomtov, Nelson.
  Haiti/Nel Yomtov.
      p. cm.—(Enchantment of the world. Second series)
  Includes bibliographical references and index.
  ISBN-13: 978-0-531-25353-3 (lib. bdg.)
  ISBN-10: 0-531-25353-8 (lib. bdg.)
  1. Haiti—Juvenile literature. I. Title. II. Series.
  F1915.2.Y66 2012
  972.94—dc22   2011010048

No part of this publication may be reproduced in whole or in part, or stored in a retrieval system, or transmitted in any form or by any means, electronic, mechanical, photocopying, recording, or otherwise, without written permission of the publisher. For information regarding permission, write to Scholastic Inc., 557 Broadway, New York, NY 10012.

© 2012 by Scholastic Inc.
All rights reserved. Published in 2012 by Children's Press, an imprint of Scholastic Inc.
Printed in the United States of America 113

SCHOLASTIC, CHILDREN'S PRESS, and associated logos are trademarks and/or registered trademarks of Scholastic Inc.
1 2 3 4 5 6 7 8 9 10 R 21 20 19 18 17 16 15 14 13 12

Haiti

Contents

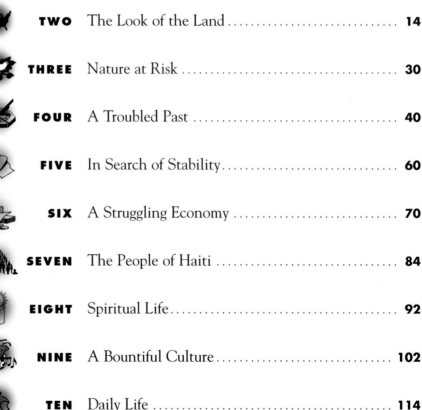

Cover photo:
Haitian woman

Cabbage field

Public bus

Courage and Hope

8

HAITI IS A PUZZLING NATION. IT IS THE POOREST country in the Western Hemisphere and one of the poorest nations in the world. The tiny Caribbean republic has suffered more than two hundred years of poverty, racism, political instability, and foreign invasion.

Yet Haiti has one of the richest histories in the Americas. The Spanish built the first European settlement in the Western Hemisphere in what is now Haiti. France soon took over the land. By 1770, Haitian plantations were more profitable than any in the United States. Haiti was also the first free black republic in the world, the result of the first and only successful slave revolution. And Haiti was only the second colony in the Western Hemisphere to declare its independence, after the United States.

Haiti's diverse cultural background includes French, African, and Caribbean influences. These can be seen in the country's food, language, art, and belief systems, especially the intriguing Vodou religion. Few nations in the world can claim such a vibrant cultural heritage.

Opposite: **A young woman at a market in Port-au-Prince, Haiti's capital city**

"Discovered"

In 1492, explorer Christopher Columbus, an Italian working for Spain, led the first European journey to the island of Hispaniola, which Haiti shares with the Dominican Republic. He described the island as being fertile and having fine harbors. "The land is high and has many ranges of hills. They are covered with tall trees of different kinds which seem to reach the sky," he wrote. The island was home to the Taino Arawak people. About five hundred thousand Tainos lived on Hispaniola. They called their land Ayiti, which means "Land of Mountains." Years later, Ayiti became Haiti.

Growth

France took control of what is now Haiti in the 1650s. They named their colony Saint-Domingue. It became a valuable producer of coffee and sugar. The French brought enslaved Africans to the colony to work on the plantations. The slaves

Christopher Columbus made his first journey to North America with three ships.

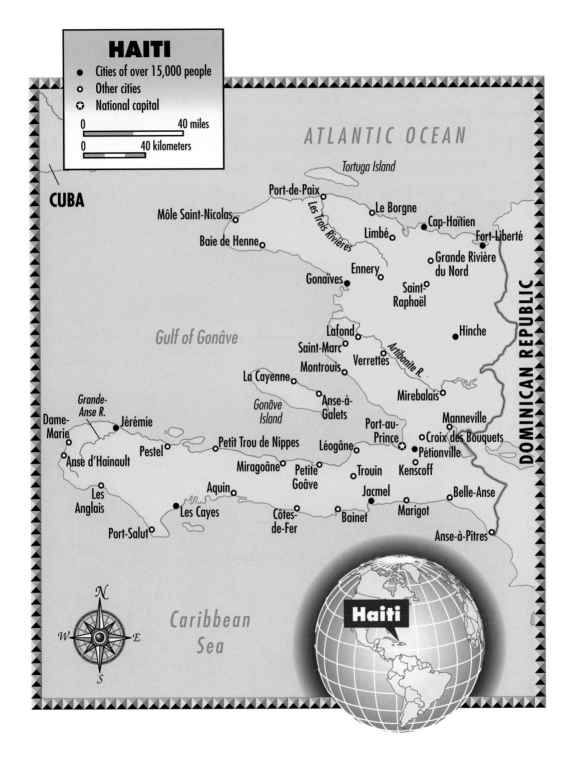

HAITI

- ● Cities of over 15,000 people
- ○ Other cities
- ✪ National capital

0   40 miles

0   40 kilometers

ATLANTIC OCEAN

Tortuga Island

CUBA

Port-de-Paix

Môle Saint-Nicolas

Baie de Henne

Les Trois Rivières

Le Borgne

Limbé

Cap-Haïtien

Fort-Liberté

Grande Rivière du Nord

Ennery

Gonaïves

Saint-Raphaël

Gulf of Gonâve

Lafond

Saint-Marc

Montrouis

Verrettes

Hinche

Artibonite R.

La Cayenne

Anse-à-Galets

Mirebalais

Gonâve Island

Manneville

Grande-Anse R.

Dame-Marie

Jérémie

Pestel

Petit Trou de Nippes

Léogâne

Port-au-Prince

Croix des Bouquets

Pétionville

Anse d'Hainault

Miragoâne

Petite Goâve

Trouin

Kenscoff

Aquin

Les Anglais

Les Cayes

Côtes-de-Fer

Bainet

Jacmel

Marigot

Belle-Anse

Port-Salut

Anse-à-Pitres

DOMINICAN REPUBLIC

N
W   E
S

Caribbean Sea

Haiti

were treated harshly, and hundreds of thousands of them died from overwork and disease.

In the 1790s, a large army of black slaves rose up against French control. They won their freedom, and the French ended slavery in the colony. In 1801, however, French leader Napoléon Bonaparte sent a new army to reestablish slavery and French dominance in the colony. Once again, the black rebels fought their oppressors and won. On January 1, 1804, Saint-Domingue officially declared its independence from France, becoming the nation of Haiti.

The High Cost of Freedom

Haiti's fight for independence came at a high price, and the republic faced many problems. The plantation system that

A sugar plantation in Haiti. The labor of enslaved Africans made many French people in Haiti wealthy.

A woman sells fruit at a market. About two-thirds of Haitians work in agriculture.

had created such great wealth was in ruins after years of fighting. The war killed about one-quarter of all the people in the colony. Nearly all the French colonists left or were killed. Other countries refused to trade with Haiti because they disapproved of the slave rebellion. Haiti faced the constant threat of foreign interference.

Today, a great divide separates rich and poor in Haiti. The wealthy few enjoy a life of abundance. The majority of Haitians, however, live in poverty and do not have enough food. Crime, unemployment, lack of health care, and devastating natural disasters have added to Haiti's miseries. Despite the enormous challenges they face, Haitians have always displayed a spirit and strength that seems unbreakable. With a strong sense of hope and great courage, they continue to work for the principles their ancestors fought for long ago: democracy, human rights, and freedom.

The Look of the Land

THE REPUBLIC OF HAITI OCCUPIES THE WESTERN THIRD of the island of Hispaniola, the second-largest island in the Caribbean Sea. The Dominican Republic makes up the rest of the island. Cuba and Jamaica lie to the west, and Puerto Rico lies to the east. Together, these islands make up the Greater Antilles, a chain of islands in the northern Caribbean.

Haiti is shaped like an open mouth, with the capital city of Port-au-Prince at the point where the two jaws meet. The jaws form a northern peninsula and a southern peninsula. The Gulf of Gonâve stretches between the two peninsulas.

Haiti's land contains large mountain ranges broken up by stretches of low-lying plains. Only about 20 percent of Haiti's land is good for farming, yet almost half of the land is cultivated. Very few forests remain because trees have been cut down for fuel and farmland.

Opposite: **Some Haitian farmers have cut steps into the land. This gives them more flat fields on which to grow crops.**

Nearby Neighbors

Haiti's closest neighbor is the Dominican Republic. The countries share a border that is 171 miles (275 kilometers) long.

Haiti's Geographic Features

Area: 10,714 square miles (27,749 sq km)

Coastline: 1,131 miles (1,820 km)

Highest Elevation: Pic la Selle, 8,793 feet (2,680 m) above sea level

Lowest Elevation: Sea level along the coast

Longest River: Artibonite River, 174 miles (280 km)

Largest Lake: Lake Saumâtre, 66 square miles (171 sq km)

Driest Months (Port-au-Prince): December and January, 1.3 inches (3.3 cm) average rainfall

Wettest Month (Port-au-Prince): May, 9 inches (23 cm) average rainfall

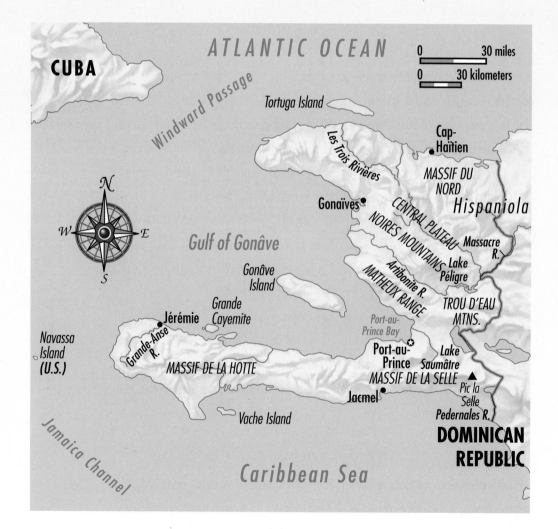

The border is formed partly by the Pedernales River in the south and the Massacre River in the north. The Dominican Republic's geography is similar to Haiti's, with plains, rocky mountain areas, and patches of farmland.

Cuba is the island closest to Haiti. Its closest point lies only 50 miles (80 km) to the northwest across a body of water called the Windward Passage.

Mountains and Plains

Mountains cover about 80 percent of Haiti. The nation's major mountain ranges include the Massif du Nord, the Massif de la Selle, and the Matheux Mountains. The Massif du Nord is the

Haiti is the most mountainous nation in the Caribbean.

The Central Plateau spreads out across north-central Haiti.

longest mountain range in the country. It runs along Haiti's northern coast and crosses into the Dominican Republic. The highest point in Haiti is the Pic la Selle, located in the Massif de la Selle range in the south. The mountain rises to 8,793 feet (2,680 meters). The Massif de la Selle becomes the Massif de la Hotte as it extends westward. The Noires Mountains and the Matheux Mountains stretch across central Haiti.

Plains and plateaus lie between the various mountain ranges. The Central Plateau stretches from the Noires Mountains to the border with the Dominican Republic. The narrow Cul-de-Sac Plain extends east from Port-au-Prince. And the North Plain lies between the Massif du Nord and the Atlantic Ocean. During the colonial period, many plantations were located on the fertile plains and plateaus.

Several islands are part of the Republic of Haiti. The largest is Gonâve Island, located northwest of Port-au-Prince in the Gulf of Gonâve. The island is 37 miles (60 km) long and 9 miles (14 km) wide. Its land is mostly dry and hilly, which makes farming almost impossible. An earthquake in 2010 destroyed the island's docks, but supplies were flown in and landed on a dirt airstrip. About seventy-five thousand people live on Gonâve.

Vache Island sits off Haiti's southwest coast. The island is small, only 8 miles (13 km) long and 2 miles (3 km) wide. Vache Island is one of the most beautiful islands in the Caribbean, and it attracts many tourists. The town of Port Morgan is named for the pirate Henry Morgan, who made many raids from his base on the island. About fifteen thousand people live on Vache Island.

Vache means "cow" in French. Vache Island got its name because it was once overrun by cows, the descendants of animals left behind by the Spanish.

Pirate Jean Le Vasseur built a fortress on Tortuga Island in the seventeenth century. Its remains still stand.

Tortuga Island, off the north coast of Haiti, was a major center of pirate activity in the mid-seventeenth century. Pirates built Fort de la Roche, on the southeast side of Tortuga, to fend off attacks from Spanish forces. Tortuga was named for its shape. In Spanish, *tortuga* means "turtle."

Grande Cayemite and Petite Cayemite are two islands off the northern coast of the southern peninsula. The beaches of Grande Cayemite offer a breathtaking view of the Massif de la Hotte on Haiti's nearby southern peninsula.

City Views

Port-au-Prince, the capital city, is Haiti's largest city, with an estimated population of 2,350,000 in 2010. Carrefour, a suburb of Port-au-Prince, is Haiti's second-largest city. In 2010, it had an estimated population of 430,250 people. Carrefour is a poor community. Most of the people who live there work in the nearby capital. The third-largest city, Delmas, which has a population of 359,451, is also a suburb of Port-au-Prince.

Pétionville (right) is located in the hills east of the capital. It is Haiti's fourth-largest city, with a population of 271,175 in 2010. Pétionville is named after Haitian general Alexandre Sabès Pétion, who was one of Haiti's founders. It is one of the wealthiest cities in Haiti. Rich Haitians make their homes there because the cool mountain temperatures make it comfortable.

Cap-Haïtien (below), the nation's fifth-largest city with a population of 155,505, lies along the

northern coast. It was an important colonial city and the capital of the Kingdom of Northern Haiti. King Henri Christophe built his palace, Sans-Souci, at the nearby town of Milot. Over the years, Cap-Haïtien has been badly damaged by earthquakes and fires, so few colonial buildings have survived.

Gonaïves, Haiti's sixth-largest city, is a seaport town on the western coast. In 1802, during the Haitian Revolution, the Battle of Ravine-à-Couleuvres was fought nearby. Gonaïves is called the "City of Independence" because it is where Haitians declared their independence from France in 1804. Gonaïves is important to Haiti's economy. Ships leave its harbors carrying products such as coffee and mangoes to other parts of Haiti and overseas.

The Artibonite River flows across central Haiti into the Gulf of Gonâve.

Rivers and Lakes

Most of Haiti's rivers are shallow, and boats cannot travel on them easily. But people use the water in rivers to irrigate crops. The Artibonite River is the longest river in Haiti—and in all of the Caribbean—running 174 miles (280 km) from east to west. It provides water to a surrounding valley, where many of Haiti's crops are grown. The Artibonite empties into the Gulf of Gonâve.

In 1956, the Péligre Dam was built on the Artibonite to produce electricity for the country. Electricity is created when water flows over turbines in a power plant. The plant was completed by 1971. Over the years, the dam has not been properly maintained, and Haiti's production of electricity has fallen by more than 30 percent since 2004.

Lake Saumâtre is Haiti's biggest lake, covering an area of 66 square miles (171 sq km). The lake lies 18 miles (29 km) east of Port-au-Prince and forms part of Haiti's border with the Dominican Republic. *Saumâtre* means "salty," and the lake is in fact brackish, or somewhat salty. The lake and the surrounding area support many animal species, including crocodiles, iguanas, flamingos, and many other kinds of birds.

The Péligre Dam is the largest dam on the island of Hispaniola.

Waves lap the shore at Jacmel, on the southern coast.

Climate

Haiti is typically hot all year. The annual average temperature is 77 degrees Fahrenheit (25 degrees Celsius) in January and 84°F (29°C) in July. It is hottest from June to September and coolest from February to April. On the coasts and in high mountain regions, temperatures are often lower.

Haiti is a relatively dry country. It lies in what's called a rain shadow. A rain shadow occurs on Hispaniola when winds from the sea push warm, moist air up the mountain slopes. As the air rises and cools, rain is produced over the Dominican Republic. When the air finally reaches Haiti, there is no more rain left to fall. Because of this, Haiti receives less rain than the Dominican Republic.

Haiti does have a rainy season in the summer. June through October is also the hurricane season, when storms over the Atlantic Ocean move into the Caribbean. In 2004, Hurricane Jeanne dumped 13 inches (33 centimeters) of rain on Haiti's northern mountain region. Floods and mudslides killed more than 3,000 people. The most damage occurred in the coastal city of Gonaïves, where four-fifths of the city's population was affected. In 2008, hurricanes Gustav, Hanna, and Ike, and tropical storm Fay struck Haiti. Heavy rains washed over the countryside and caused enormous destruction. About 1,700

Three hurricanes struck Haiti in 2008, leaving thousands of houses in ruins.

In 2010, Haitians planted thousands of trees on the steep slopes of northern Haiti. Trees prevent mudslides by keeping the soil in place.

people were killed, injured, or went missing. The storms destroyed more than twenty-two thousand homes and damaged another eighty-five thousand. The floods washed out 70 percent of Haiti's crops. With so much food lost, hundreds of people died from hunger.

Human activity has damaged the environment in ways that make hurricanes more deadly. Almost all of Haiti's forests have been cut down so that the wood can be used as fuel. Without trees on the mountain slopes, rainwater washes rapidly downward, causing floods and mudslides that kill people and destroy property. Although millions of trees have been planted in Haiti, millions of others are cut down every year. To ease the damage caused by hurricanes, Haiti will have to replant forests and find new sources of energy and fuel.

Deadly Earthquake

At 4:53 PM on January 12, 2010, a massive earthquake struck about 15 miles (24 km) southwest of Port-au-Prince. The disaster affected an estimated 3 million people, or about one-third of Haiti's total population. An estimated 316,000 people were killed and another 300,000 were injured. The government estimates that the earthquake left 1.5 million people homeless, and destroyed fifty thousand homes and thirty thousand other buildings. Port-au-Prince was one of the hardest-hit areas. The quake destroyed the Presidential Palace, the National Assembly building, city hall, and other important landmarks.

Rubble covered much of Port-au-Prince after the 2010 earthquake.

The 2010 earthquake severely damaged an estimated 250,000 buildings.

Governments and organizations from around the world quickly rushed to Haiti's aid. They contributed money, rescue and medical teams, food, water, and equipment. But the damage done by the quake slowed their efforts. Haiti's main airport and seaport had been destroyed. Roads were blocked and telephone service was not available. Supplies and rescue teams could not reach the people of Haiti. With their homes in ruins, tens of thousands of Haitians moved to other places. Many went to other parts of Haiti. Others fled to foreign countries such as the United States, Canada, and the Dominican Republic.

One year after the earthquake, the situation still looked grim. About 1.6 million people were living in tents in large camps. Many camps had no running water, electricity, or systems for disposing of waste and garbage. Only 5 percent of the rubble around the country had been cleared, and only 15 percent of the necessary temporary houses had been built. An outbreak of the deadly disease cholera, which is spread by contaminated food and water, killed thousands of Haitians.

The people of Haiti have continued to suffer. Some wonder if their nation will ever recover from the tragedy.

Solar-Powered Relief

Haiti faces a serious energy shortage. Oil is expensive and hard to obtain. Only about 13 percent of the population has electricity. When the 2010 earthquake struck, lots of energy was needed to help the recovery. Scientists and engineers turned to solar power as part of the solution. Solar power captures sunlight and turns it into electricity.

Companies around the world donated solar equipment to Haiti. Solar-powered equipment was used to pump water from beneath the ground to provide quake victims with drinking and bathing water. Solar-powered streetlights were set up to help the rescue effort after dark. Relief workers were given cell phones powered by solar energy so they could communicate and coordinate their efforts. Solar-powered ovens were set up to provide healthy meals without electricity. Laptop computers that run on solar energy were given to schools so students could use the Internet and continue their education. It is hoped that the solar-powered equipment will make the lives of Haitians easier long into the future.

Nature at Risk

W HEN CHRISTOPHER COLUMBUS SET FOOT ON THE island of Hispaniola in 1492, he found lush, green countryside. More than 90 percent of the land was forested. In 1923, 60 percent of the land remained forested. Today, less than 2 percent of Haiti is forested land.

The people in Haiti have been cutting down trees for hundreds of years. This deforestation has eliminated nearly all the trees on the island. Following independence from colonial rule, huge tracts of trees were removed from the plantations to create farmland for the growing population. In recent decades, people have cut down trees for use as building materials and cooking fuel. The wood is essential to daily life in Haiti.

Deforestation causes the topsoil to wash away. This makes the soil less healthy, so that plants and trees do not grow as well. Pine and hardwood trees now grow only in the upper reaches of the mountains. In the 1980s, Haitian farmers planted more than 25 million trees, but even those could not keep pace with the continuing deforestation of the country.

Opposite: **Trees surround the Saut d'Eau waterfall in central Haiti. In most parts of the country, however, trees have been cut down.**

Flowering plants brighten the Haitian landscape.

Plant Life

Mangrove trees grow along the Gulf of Gonâve on the northwest coast and on the Atlantic coast near Cap-Haïtien. Mangroves are unusual in that they can grow in saltwater. Their tall, thin roots rise above the surface of the water. Below the surface, the tree roots provide shelter for many types of fish, oysters, and other sea creatures. Mangroves, however, are harvested for wood and are quickly disappearing as well. Without them, the creatures living among the mangrove roots will disappear, too.

Roughly 5,600 species of plants grow in Haiti. Guava fruit grows in large thickets along the coastline. Europeans prob-

Preserving Nature

Pic Macaya (Makaya Peak) National Park is located in the Massif de la Hotte mountain range in the southern part of Haiti. The goals of the park, which was established in 1983, include preserving Haiti's natural habitats and providing technical advice to Haitian communities about protecting the environment. Pic Macaya is one of the very few natural forests in Haiti that conserves the plant and animal life of the region. It includes many endangered species, including some that exist only in Haiti. It also features Haiti's last uncut cloud forest, an evergreen forest that is covered by low-level clouds at almost all times of the year.

ably first encountered pineapples on Hispaniola. Mangoes are also common.

Tropical flowers such as royal poincianas, poinsettias, frangipani, and bougainvillea offer beauty and fragrance where they blossom. About twenty species of plants grow only in Haiti. These include an orchid called tomzanonia and a tree fern called *Cyathea hotteana* that grows 6 feet (2 m) tall.

Sea Creatures

Coral reefs provide a home for hundreds of species of sea life in and around Haiti. Reefs are rocklike formations that are made from the skeletons of tiny creatures called polyps. Many kinds of sea creatures live near coral reefs. The fairy basslet, the queen angelfish, the rock beauty, and the blue tang are some of the more colorful fish that live near coral reefs. Fishers harvest lobsters and conch from shallow reefs. The

The manatee eats only plants. It spends about half its life eating.

reefs around Haiti are in danger from human activity. Heavily populated coastal zones and high unemployment has resulted in the reefs being overfished as a way to provide food and jobs. Oil pollution and solid waste settling near coastal zones also put reefs at risk.

The West Indian manatee inhabits the coastal areas of Hispaniola. Manatees generally grow to about 10 feet (3 m) long and can weigh up to 1,300 pounds (600 kilograms). They

Flying Mammals

Haiti is home to about fourteen different species of bats, including the Mexican free-tailed bat. The Mexican free-tailed bat is about 3.5 inches (9 cm) long and weighs less than half an ounce (14 grams). When the mother bat leaves its cave to hunt for food, she leaves her babies behind. She finds her way back to the babies by recognizing their unique smell and cry. Bats are the world's only flying mammals, and they make up about 20 percent of all mammal species in the world.

feed on sea grasses and plant leaves. Manatees are slow moving and swim near the surface. This means that they are easily struck by boats or propellers. Hunting and an increase in boat traffic have made the manatee highly endangered.

Turtles living off Hispaniola's coast include the leatherback, the loggerhead, the hawksbill, and the green sea turtle. The leatherback is the world's largest sea turtle. Adults can grow up to 6.5 feet long (2 m) and weigh as much as 1,500 pounds (680 kg). They feed almost entirely on jellyfish. Near Hispaniola, the hawksbill lives mostly among the reefs, feeding on sea sponges. Since ancient times, people have used the hawksbill's colorful shell as decoration.

Birds

Roughly 260 species of birds have been recorded on Haiti. Among them are 22 species of sandpipers, 12 species of terns, and 11 species of pigeons and doves. Twenty-nine species of

The National Bird

The Hispaniolan trogon is the national bird of Haiti. It measures about 12 inches (30 cm) long and has shiny green wings, a red belly, and a gray throat and breast. Its long tail is dark blue with white markings. The Hispaniolan trogon lives in the forests of the southwestern Massif de la Hotte mountain range. It feeds on insects, fruits, and small lizards.

birds exist only on Haiti. They include the bay-breasted cuckoo, the ashy-faced owl, and the Hispaniolan emerald hummingbird.

Ridgway's hawk is another bird found only on Hispaniola. Standing about 1 foot (30 cm) tall, it feeds on small mammals, lizards, and snakes. Like many birds in the region, it is endangered because the forests where it lives have been cut down.

Ten species of egrets and flamingos inhabit the island. Many of them nest near Lake Saumâtre on the Cul-de-Sac Plain, which extends from Port-au-Prince to the Dominican Republic. They include the great blue heron, the tricolored heron, and the snowy and cattle egrets. These birds feed mainly on fish, shellfish, and small reptiles.

Reptiles and Amphibians

The rhinoceros iguana is a species of lizard found only on Hispaniola. It varies in size from 2 to 4.5 feet (60 to 140 cm) long. Adults can weigh as much as 20 pounds (9 kg). The male rhinoceros iguana has a bony growth on its snout, which looks like three horns. The bony growth provides protection.

Although the rhinoceros iguana looks fearsome, it is very shy. It eats leaves, flowers, fruits, and berries.

The American crocodile population in Hispaniola is one of the largest wild crocodile populations in the world. Females grow to about 8 feet (2.5 m) long, and males can grow to about 13 feet (4 m) long. Their diets consist of fish, turtles, and occasionally dogs or goats.

American crocodiles hunt by sitting still in the water. When prey comes near, the crocodile grabs it and drowns it.

Aiding the Animals

The Animal Relief Coalition for Haiti (ARCH) is a group of animal protection agencies in Haiti, which aids animals affected by the 2010 earthquake. The group is providing health care for many thousands of injured, homeless, diseased, or starving creatures. By January 2011, ARCH had treated fifty thousand animals. The patients included dogs, cats, horses, cattle, pigs, goats, and sheep.

ARCH works closely with the government to train Haitian animal doctors. It has also begun a program of giving vaccinations to protect people and animals from diseases such as rabies and anthrax.

Frogs are common in Haiti, which is home to about forty-nine species. Among the rarest are the Macaya breast-spot frog and the Hispaniolan ventriloquial frog. The Macaya breast-spot is found in Massif de la Hotte. It is one of the world's smallest frogs, with adults growing only to about the size of a grape. The Hispaniolan ventriloquial frog is a burrowing frog that makes a rapid chirping sound of seven different notes. Their habitats are disappearing as trees are cut down, so both species are highly endangered.

Land Mammals

The Hispaniolan hutia and the Haitian solenodon are two mammals that live only on Hispaniola. The hutia is a medium-sized rodent that grows to about 13 inches (33 cm) long. It lives in forests, often in tree trunks. Their numbers are declining because deforestation threatens their habitat. Hutias are also becoming less common because they are hunted for food, both by the mongoose, a small catlike animal, and by humans.

The Haitian solenodon is a shrewlike mammal that measures about 13 inches (33 cm) long. It has strong claws that it uses to dig around roots in search of food. It feeds mainly on worms, snails, fruit, and small reptiles. The solenodon's bite is poisonous and can even be fatal, making it one of only a few venomous mammals in the world.

Hutias are most active at night. They feed on fruit, leaves, and twigs.

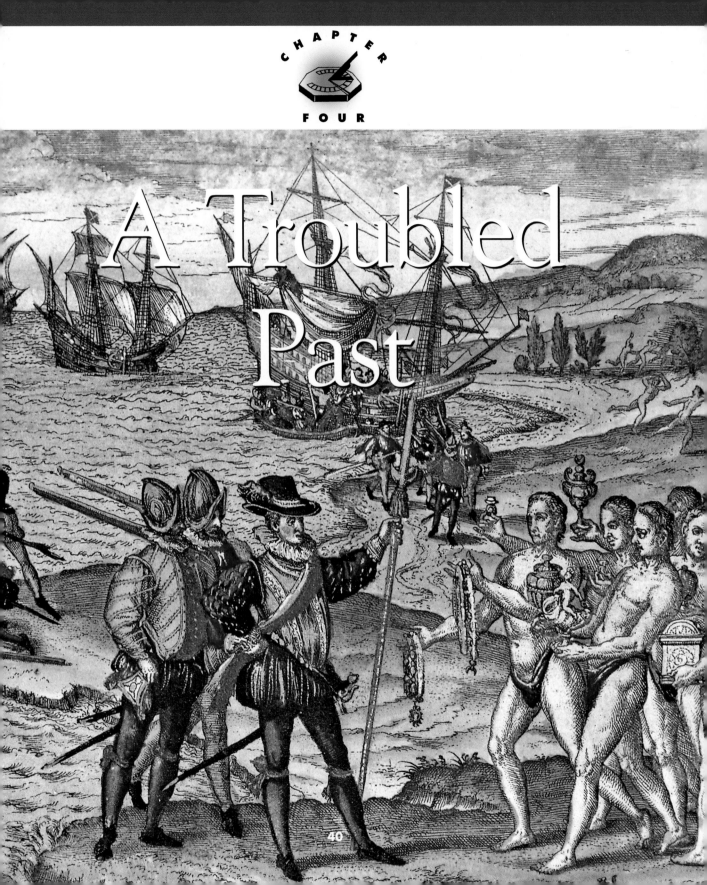

A Troubled Past

WHEN CHRISTOPHER COLUMBUS LANDED ON Hispaniola on December 5, 1492, he had no idea how important his "discovery" would be. Four months earlier, Columbus had sailed from Spain with a crew of nearly ninety men aboard three ships. They were seeking a quick, safe water route to Asia, where gold, silk, and other valuable items were available for trade.

Hispaniola was one of the first places Columbus came to when he stumbled upon the Western Hemisphere. The Taino Arawak people living on Hispaniola were friendly to the Europeans, and they gave the strangers gifts of gold ornaments. This led Columbus to think the island was rich with this valuable treasure. He and his men built a small fort called La Navidad ("Christmas" in Spanish) to house themselves. When Columbus set off on the return journey to Spain in January 1493, he left thirty-nine sailors at La Navidad. He gave them orders to look for gold and promised them he would return to pick them up.

When Columbus arrived back in Hispaniola in November 1493, he found the fort in ruins. The Tainos had killed all

Opposite: **The Taino Arawak people who lived on Hispaniola greeted Columbus and his crew warmly.**

A sugar plantation in the colony of Saint-Domingue. During the 1700s, Saint-Domingue produced 40 percent of the sugar used in Europe.

the sailors. Columbus forced the native people to work for the Spanish, planting crops and looking for gold. He also established a colony called Santo Domingo. Although Spain claimed all of Hispaniola, it colonized only the eastern portion for the next hundred years.

Eventually, more Spanish settlers arrived on Hispaniola and set up large sugar plantations, where they forced the Tainos to work. By the mid-sixteenth century, the endless labor, the landowners' cruelty, and European diseases slashed the native population from five hundred thousand to five thousand.

Now, faced with a labor shortage, the Spaniards began bringing people to Haiti from Africa to work as slaves.

The Spanish were not alone in their desire to colonize and control the potential riches of the Americas. By the early 1600s, French settlers established villages and farms on the northwestern tip of the island. In 1697, the Treaty of Ryswick between France and Spain officially divided Hispaniola. France was given the western third of the island, and Spain the eastern two-thirds. The French named their portion Saint-Domingue. This region later became Haiti. The Spanish retained the name Santo Domingo. It later became the Dominican Republic.

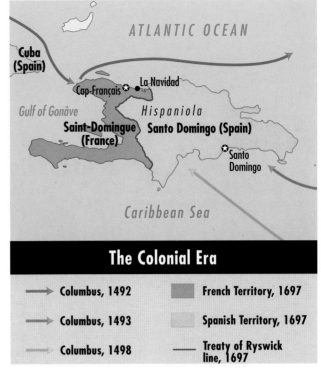

The Colonial Era

→ Columbus, 1492
→ Columbus, 1493
→ Columbus, 1498

▮ French Territory, 1697
▯ Spanish Territory, 1697
— Treaty of Ryswick line, 1697

Wealth and Inequality

Saint-Domingue rapidly prospered. By the mid-1700s, the French had established huge plantations of sugarcane, coffee, cotton, and indigo. Millions of pounds of these products were exported each year. The tiny colony had become essential to France's existence as a powerful European nation.

An enormous labor force, made entirely of enslaved people imported from Africa, worked the plantations. Buying slaves was expensive, but the plantations were so profitable that it was worth it to the plantation owners. They paid about US$25,000

A Borrowed Language

Several words in the English language are borrowed from the Taino Arawak language. They include:

hamaca	hammock
sabana	savanna
canoa	canoe
barbacoa	barbeque
huracan	hurricane
tabaco	tobacco

A slave market in Saint-Domingue. Thousands of Africans were kidnapped and shipped to Saint-Domingue to be sold as slaves.

in today's money for a person who had been kidnapped and sold into slavery. That's what many new cars cost today.

In 1789, there were roughly five hundred thousand enslaved people in Haiti. A white population of about thirty-nine thousand controlled the slaves. Some colonists were wealthy plantation owners. Most were from France, but some had been born on Hispaniola. They were called Creoles. Mulattoes, or people with both black and white ancestors, numbered twenty-four thousand. Some mulattoes were well educated and wealthy, owning property and slaves. Some were free but poor; still others were enslaved.

Throughout much of the eighteenth century, Maroons, or escaped slaves, fled the brutality of the plantations. They escaped into the mountains on the outskirts of Saint-Domingue's towns. They sometimes raided isolated plantations for food and supplies.

In the late eighteenth century, word of the French Revolution's decree that "Men are born and remain free and equal" reached the New World. Mulattoes and blacks took these words to heart. White landowners responded by instituting a series of laws that limited the rights of rich mulattoes.

A French lady travels in a horse-drawn carriage in Saint-Domingue. The wealthy relied on slave labor to keep the same comforts they had back in France.

On August 14, 1791, Vodou priest Dutty Boukman addressed a gathering of enslaved people outside the city of Cap-Haïtien. He rallied the crowd to revolt and called for the death of their oppressors. A week later, tens of thousands of slaves rose up against their owners. Armed with machetes, farm tools, and torches, they burned hundreds of plantations and killed two thousand whites. To ease the violence, France sent six thousand soldiers to Saint-Domingue, but they failed to halt the rebellion.

Carefully watching the situation in Saint-Domingue, the Spanish plotted to win control of the western part of Hispaniola. They threw their support to the rebellious slaves

The largest slave uprising ever to take place in the Americas began on the night of August 21, 1791. It was the beginning of the struggle for Haitian independence.

and, in 1793, took control of northern and central Saint-Domingue. François Dominique Toussaint, an educated former slave who had joined the rebellion, was one of the leaders of the black forces for Spain. But after February 1794, when France abolished slavery in the colony, Toussaint decided to support the French instead and joined the French army. He fought other black leaders who were loyal to Spain and restored control of most of Saint-Domingue to the French.

After 1794, Toussaint began calling himself Louverture, which means "the opening." From then on, he would be known as Toussaint Louverture.

Louverture believed Saint-Domingue should stay connected to France, but he wanted to end white colonial rule. From 1795 to 1799, he used both political and military tactics

Parts of Cap-Français, which would later be renamed Cap-Haïtien, burned during the fighting in 1793.

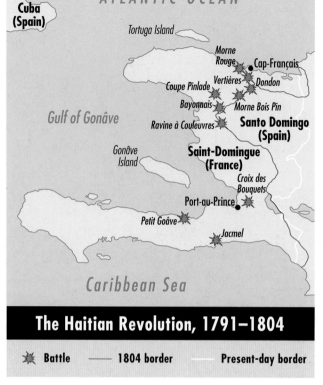

ATLANTIC OCEAN

Cuba (Spain)

Tortuga Island

Morne Rouge

Cap-Français

Vertières

Dondon

Coupe Pinlade

Bayonnais

Morne Bois Pin

Gulf of Gonâve

Ravine à Couleuvres

Santo Domingo (Spain)

Gonâve Island

Saint-Domingue (France)

Croix des Bouquets

Port-au-Prince

Petit Goâve

Jacmel

Caribbean Sea

The Haitian Revolution, 1791–1804

✳ Battle —— 1804 border —— Present-day border

to drive the French leaders back to France. He became the most powerful man in Saint-Domingue.

Louverture set up a new system of government. He declared himself governor for life and took the power to make all laws, appoint government officials, and control Saint-Domingue's finances. He declared that slavery was forever abolished and set about to rebuild a land that had been torn apart by a decade of violence. Under his leadership, Saint-Domingue achieved important goals, such as restoring the productivity of coffee plantations.

Rebel Leader

François Dominique Toussaint was born in 1743 on a plantation in northern Saint-Domingue. A black freedman named Pierre Baptiste probably taught him how to read and write. Baptiste also taught him about the medicinal properties of plants and herbs. Toussaint was nicknamed the Physician by the slaves he cared for.

After revolt erupted in 1791, Toussaint joined his fellow slaves and became a brilliant military leader. After 1794, he started to call himself Louverture, which means "the opening." Many historians believe he took this name to show his determination to launch a new era of freedom.

He led black troops under the French flag and defeated the Spanish. From 1798 until his capture in 1802, he was the colony's most important leader. He died in a French prison on April 7, 1803.

In 1799, Napoléon Bonaparte seized control of the French government. He was thirty years old at the time.

In 1802, General Napoléon Bonaparte of France turned his attention to Saint-Domingue with the goal of reestablishing slavery. Over the course of about a year, he sent more than forty thousand troops to take control of the colony. Louverture knew he could not defeat a force of that size. He gave instructions to Haitians to burn towns and retreat into the mountains.

The islanders fought bravely, but they were unable to defeat the French force. In May 1802, Louverture agreed to surrender. He was sent to prison in France and died less than one year later.

Jean-Jacques Dessalines was the first leader of an independent Haiti. In this painting by Philomé Obin, one of Haiti's greatest artists, he is shown at the front of a group of horsemen.

Independence

Jean-Jacques Dessalines, Louverture's strongest ally, became the leader of the revolution. After several victories against the French, Dessalines's troops finally dealt them a crushing blow at the Battle of Vertières in November 1803. The victory ended France's attempts at defeating the revolution and reestablishing slavery.

On January 1, 1804, Dessalines declared Haiti an independent nation. Yet the bloodshed continued when Dessalines ordered the army to massacre thousands of French colonists. Haiti's first constitution, approved in May 1805, gave Dessalines total governing power. He declared himself emperor and established Haiti as a military dictatorship, as it had been under Louverture.

Slavery had been abolished, but Dessalines continued Louverture's system of *fermage* (tenant farming). Under this system, the government took control of land and rented it to army officers or other officials. Former slaves were then made to work the fields under military supervision. This form of forced labor and Dessalines's inability to improve the economy led to an uprising. Dessalines was assassinated in October 1806. Leadership of the new nation was once again up for grabs.

Southern and northern Haitians could not agree upon a new leader. A

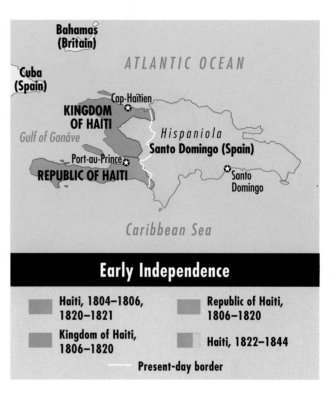

Early Independence

Haiti, 1804–1806, 1820–1821	Republic of Haiti, 1806–1820
Kingdom of Haiti, 1806–1820	Haiti, 1822–1844

—— Present-day border

Citadelle Laferrière

In 1805, General Henri Christophe ordered the construction of a large citadel, or fortress, on a mountaintop in northern Haiti. If French troops tried to retake Haiti, Henri Christophe and his troops would be able to retreat to the citadel and defend themselves.

Henri Christophe's Citadelle Laferrière is the largest fortress in the Western Hemisphere. Its walls are 13 feet (4 m) thick and reach heights of 130 feet (40 m). To build the citadel, thousands of people had to drag huge stones up a mountain peak that was 3,000 feet (900 m) high. Today, the Citadelle Laferrière is the most recognized landmark in Haiti.

General Henri Christophe was one of Toussaint Louverture's lieutenants during Haiti's war for independence.

short civil war between the two sides did not settle the issue. For the next twenty years, General Henri Christophe ruled as king in the north. General Alexandre Pétion, followed by Jean-Pierre Boyer, ruled a democratic state in the south. Christophe's northern kingdom was mostly black. The republic in the south was mulatto. When Christophe died in 1820, Boyer peacefully reunited the north and south. He soon invaded Santo Domingo and took over the entire island.

Road to Ruin

Under Boyer's rule, Haiti fell into economic, physical, and diplomatic ruin. Race distinctions became more prominent. This resulted in a government and economy run by mulattoes and a military controlled by blacks. Boyer was overthrown by the military in 1843.

Soon after, a revolution in Santo Domingo erupted. This eventually led to "Spanish Haiti" declaring its independence and becoming the Dominican Republic.

Between 1843 and 1915, Haiti had twenty different leaders. Violent revolts and widening racial and socioeconomic divisions continued to plague the nation. Many other countries refused to trade with Haiti because they believed the people were wrong to rebel against slavery. This made it difficult for the leaders of the young nation to develop its economy. Foreign nations, including France, Germany, England, and the United States, dominated Haiti's import and export businesses. Eventually, the United States would occupy Haiti to protect its own interests.

Port-au-Prince in 1901. The city has been the capital since 1770.

U.S. troops march across Haiti. American forces were in Haiti from 1915 to 1934, the longest U.S. occupation of a foreign land in history.

U.S. Invasion

As Haiti faced continuing political instability, the United States kept a watchful eye on developments there. In 1914, after ten years of construction, the Panama Canal opened. The canal cuts across Central America, providing a short water route for ships traveling between the Atlantic and Pacific Oceans. They no longer had to go all the way around the southern tip of South America.

World War I began in 1914. Although the United States did not become involved in the war at first, the U.S. government knew that it might enter the war against Germany. Fearful that Germany would take control of Haiti, the United States took action to defend its interests and ensure that no other nation could block access to the Panama Canal.

In July 1915, U.S. president Woodrow Wilson sent an invasion force of marines to Haiti. Haitians did not welcome the military occupation. Large Haitian uprisings were met with overwhelming U.S. force. American marines killed thousands of Haitians. The occupying forces disbanded the Haitian army and replaced it with a well-trained, American-led military force. The United States put in place a new constitution that allowed huge international companies to buy up the best land in Haiti.

Although the United States had new roads, bridges, airports, and telephone systems built during the occupation, the U.S. presence in Haiti led to frequent riots and strikes. Because of the violence, and the growing public opinion in the United States against the occupation, U.S. troops withdrew in 1934, two years earlier than planned. Even after the marines left, Americans for a time kept control of the Haitian National Bank, railroads, power plants, and sugar refineries.

Charlemagne Péralte (front row, third from right), a military officer, led the Haitian resistance to the U.S. occupation.

In 1946, the Haitian National Assembly elected Dumarsais Estimé president. A powerful military group forced him from power in 1950 when he tried to lengthen his term of office. Paul Magloire, the leader of the military group, replaced Estimé. Magloire ruled until 1956, before, he too, was overthrown. During his term in office, Magloire had helped turn Haiti into a popular tourist spot.

In 1964, François "Papa Doc" Duvalier declared himself president for life.

In 1957, François "Papa Doc" Duvalier was elected president with the help of the military. Duvalier was a doctor and had supervised several programs to eliminate tropical diseases in Haiti. Realizing that the strength of the military could also bring him down, Duvalier got rid of the military's top leaders. In their place, he created the feared Tontons Macoutes, a gang of thugs who murdered as many as sixty thousand Haitians during the long years the Duvalier family ruled

A Reign of Terror

In 1959, François "Papa Doc" Duvalier created a violent military force called the Tontons Macoutes. Their name came from a Haitian myth about a bogeyman who kidnaps and punishes young children. Most of the members of the group came from poor rural communities. Others were criminals or former soldiers. At one time, there were as many as three hundred thousand Macoutes in Haiti. Each wore dark sunglasses, jeans, a bandana, and a peasant hat, and carried a pistol. The Macoutes patrolled the countryside torturing, kidnapping, and killing any Haitian they suspected of being disloyal to Duvalier. Fearing for their safety, thousands of wealthy Haitians fled the country. Peasant families fled to the cities, adding to the overcrowded conditions and poverty in the slums. It is estimated that the Macoutes killed as many as sixty thousand people.

Haiti. Duvalier encouraged the Macoutes to brutally eliminate any opposition to his regime.

Duvalier convinced the United States that he would fight the spread of communism in the region if the United States provided financial aid to Haiti. The Americans agreed, but most of the money went directly to Duvalier and his family. Newly established taxes and deductions from workers' paychecks also went into Duvalier's pockets. When Duvalier died in 1971, his son, Jean-Claude "Baby Doc" Duvalier, became president. Jean-Claude Duvalier's time in office was marked by alternating periods of calm and brutality. He was forced to flee Haiti in 1986. Thirty years of Duvalier dictatorship had finally ended.

A new constitution was adopted in March 1987, offering hope for Haiti's future. The constitution established a new structure for the Haitian government. It provided for a president, a prime minister, and a two-chamber legislature. After two failed attempts at fair voting and several military takeovers of the government, Haitians elected the popular Jean-Bertrand Aristide president in December 1990. Aristide launched a program of widespread reform. Yet in September 1991, he was forced to leave the country by another military takeover. The military allowed Aristide to return to office in 1994, but Haiti's bad economic situation forced him to abandon his programs to ease poverty.

Aristide's ally René Préval won the presidential election in December 1995. Préval lost voter support because food and

Priest and President

Jean-Bertrand Aristide was born on July 15, 1953, in Port-Salut, on the southern coast of Haiti. Roman Catholic priests educated him, and he became a priest himself in 1982. He strongly opposed Duvalier and was an outspoken voice for poor Haitians. Because of his work, several attempts were made to kill him. In 1990, he won the presidential election by a wide margin, but for a time he was forced out of office by the military. In 2000, he was elected again, but he was overthrown once more in 2004. In 2011, after many years of living in exile, he was finally able to return to Haiti.

fuel prices rose. Haitians also objected to Préval's proposed cutbacks in the number of government workers. In 2000, Aristide was elected once again. Opposition to his administration grew because he could not reduce the nation's poverty or effectively combat criminal gangs. In February 2004, a mob of rebels forced him to flee the country. When a new election was held in 2006, Préval was again elected president.

The next presidential election was postponed because of the massive earthquake that rocked Haiti and destroyed much of Port-au-Prince in January 2010. When the final votes were tallied in the spring of 2011, Michel Martelly had won. Martelly is a popular singer who is more conservative than Haiti's other recent presidents.

Haitian women stand in line, waiting to cast their ballots in the 2011 presidential election.

Haitians have endured a past filled with struggle and political violence and face economic and social challenges in the years ahead. They continue to work to achieve a stable democracy and hope to bring freedom and prosperity to everyone in their island home.

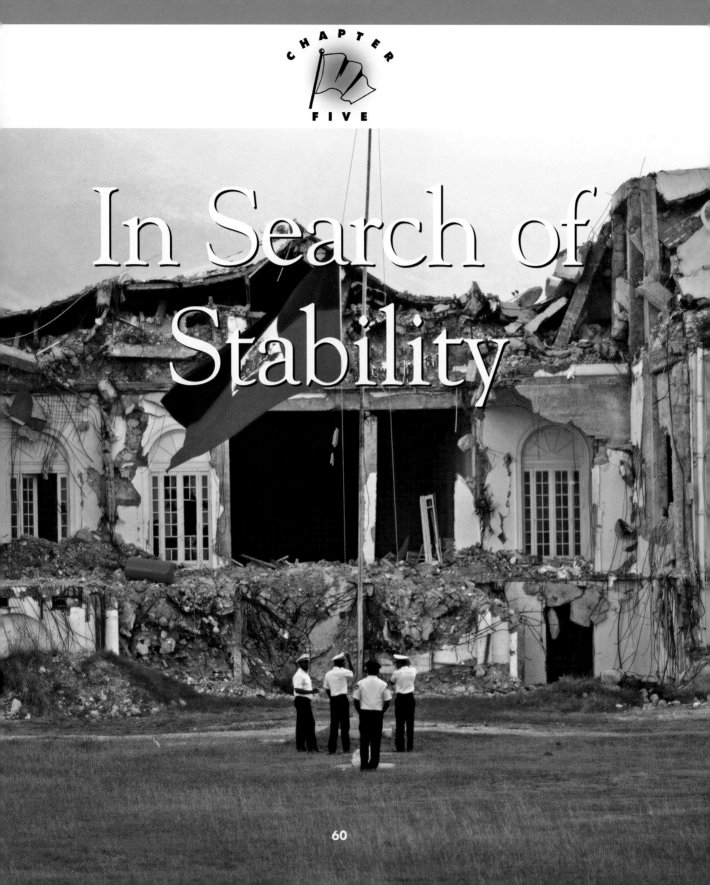

In Search of Stability

THE STORY OF HAITI'S TROUBLED DEMOCRACY DATES BACK to the days when the republic was first created. The successful slave rebellion of 1791–1804 resulted in the formation of the world's first black republic. In the two hundred years since its independence, Haiti's governments have been overthrown thirty-two times. There have been twenty-two constitutions. Several of Haiti's leaders were assassinated. Others were forced to resign, and some quit before their term of office was over. From 1988 to 1993, Haiti had twelve different governments.

Despite its unstable past, Haiti has continued to work toward creating a successful democracy. In March 1987, the current constitution was approved. It was based on the constitutions of the United States and France. Haiti's constitution divides the government into three main bodies: the executive branch, the legislative branch, and the judicial branch.

Executive Branch

The executive branch includes the president, the prime minister, and the Council of Ministers. The president is the head

Opposite: **The Presidential Palace in Port-au-Prince was destroyed in the 2010 earthquake.**

Haiti's Flag

Haiti's flag was officially adopted on May 18, 1803. Haitian revolutionary leader Jean-Jacques Dessalines is said to have created its design. He removed the white stripe of a French tricolored flag and had his goddaughter, Catherine Flon, sew together the remaining blue and red pieces. The flag signifies the union of Haiti's blacks, represented by the blue stripe, and mulattoes, represented by the red stripe. In 1964, President François Duvalier altered the flag, changing it to a black-and-red design. When his son, President Jean-Claude Duvalier, fled Haiti in February 1986, Haitians brought back the original flag.

In the center of the flag is a coat of arms on a white background that features a palm tree (a traditional symbol of liberty) with a stocking "liberty" cap

atop it. Three Haitian flags appear on each side of the tree. Below are two cannons that are set above a banner bearing the motto *L'Union fait la force* ("In union there is strength").

of state. The president is elected for a five-year term and may not serve two terms in a row. The president has many duties, as well as the power to declare war and sign treaties.

The prime minister is the head of government and is chosen by the president. The National Assembly must approve the president's choice. The prime minister is responsible for enforcing Haiti's laws and working with the president to supervise the national defense.

The Council of Ministers oversees the various government departments, or ministries. The prime minister appoints a minister to run each of these departments. Currently, there are twelve ministries, including the Ministry of Agriculture, the Ministry of Finance, the Ministry of Education, and nine others.

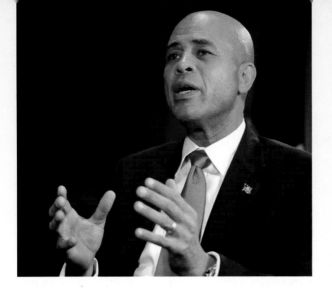

A New President

On March 20, 2011, Michel Martelly was elected president of Haiti, defeating Mirlande Manigat. Better known as "Sweet Mickey," Martelly is a popular musician who plays *kompa* music. Kompa is a style of dance music sung in the Haitian Creole language. Martelly supported the overthrow of Jean-Bertrand Aristide in 1991 and 1994. He plans to reinstitute the military that Aristide broke up in 1995.

The Legislative Branch

The legislative branch of Haiti's government is called the National Assembly. It consists of two parts, the Chamber of Deputies and the Senate. They are both responsible for making Haiti's laws.

The Chamber of Deputies has ninety-nine members. They serve four-year terms and can be reelected. The Senate has thirty members. Three members are elected from each of Haiti's ten sections, which are called departments. The deputies are elected to six-year terms, and there is no limit on the number of terms they can serve. One of the Senate's duties is to recommend judges for the Supreme

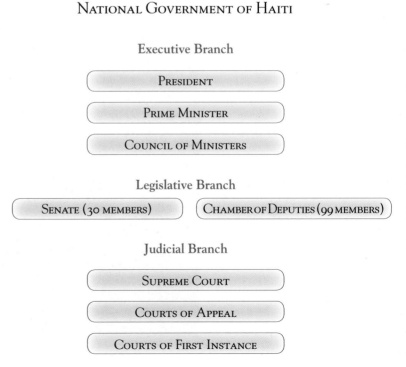

NATIONAL GOVERNMENT OF HAITI

Executive Branch

PRESIDENT

PRIME MINISTER

COUNCIL OF MINISTERS

Legislative Branch

SENATE (30 MEMBERS)

CHAMBER OF DEPUTIES (99 MEMBERS)

Judicial Branch

SUPREME COURT

COURTS OF APPEAL

COURTS OF FIRST INSTANCE

Court. It also has the power to act as a court in case a top political office holder is accused of a crime.

Both the legislative and executive branches may propose laws, but the executive branch has sole power to propose financial laws.

Judicial Branch

The judicial branch consists of the Supreme Court, the Courts of Appeal, the Courts of First Instance, and lower courts.

The president appoints all judges in the higher courts. Supreme Court judges and Courts of Appeal judges serve ten years. Courts of First Instance judges serve seven years. These courts handle the most important legal cases, including

Supreme Court justices work in the Palace of Justice. The court's justices are appointed by the president.

criminal cases. Local courts often handle cases that deal with property rights, labor conflicts, and young people who have committed crimes.

Trials are sometimes held in jails in an attempt to make the judicial process move more quickly.

A Failed System

Haiti's judicial system faces many problems. In the United States, the government provides a lawyer to a person who has been accused of a crime and must appear in court. In Haiti, the government is not required to provide lawyers, so many poor people accused of crimes do not have lawyers to represent them. Judges and witnesses are often bribed during trials. Others are threatened with physical violence.

In Search of Stability **65**

A Look at the Capital

Port-au-Prince, the capital of Haiti, is located on the Gulf of Gonâve along the southwestern coast of Haiti. Port-au-Prince was founded in 1749 and became the colonial capital in 1770. It remained the capital when Haiti declared its independence in 1804.

When the 2010 earthquake struck Port-au-Prince, the city was almost entirely destroyed. Many government buildings, including the Presidential Palace, the Legislative Palace, and the Palace of Justice, came toppling down. The airport and seaport were also badly damaged. Shipments of supplies to help the people of Port-au-Prince could not be delivered. Electrical and telephone services were lost, and fires burned out of control. Thousands and thousands of people in the Haitian city were killed or injured.

Many nations rushed to help in the relief efforts. More than US$10 billion in aid was promised, and more than ten thousand organizations offered to assist. But the recovery was slow. One year after the quake, more than one million people in Port-au-Prince were living in tents (below left). It will take many years and much hard work to rebuild the city.

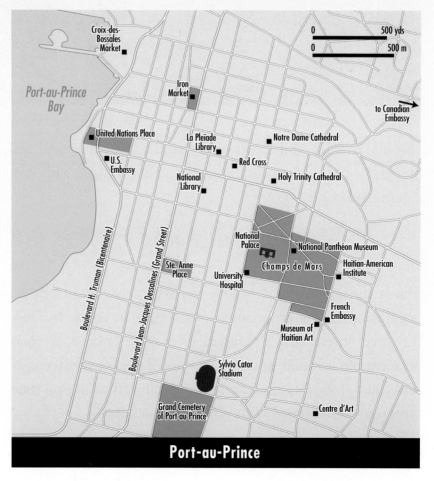

Port-au-Prince

Port-au-Prince at a Glance

Population (2010 est.): 2,350,000

Ethnic population:

93% black

5% mulatto

1% white

1% Arab and others

Founded: 1749

Elevation: Sea level

Average high temperature: 95°F (35°C) in July; 89°F (32°C) in January

Average annual precipitation: 53 inches (135 cm)

The 2010 earthquake destroyed thousands of buildings. Haitians are clearing the rubble, but it is going slowly.

New police agents salute at their graduation ceremony in 2008. They were trained by United Nations police officers.

In the late 1990s, the United States helped improve Haiti's judicial system. A program called the Administration of Justice (AOJ) offered free legal assistance to thousands of poor Haitians. It also helped free hundreds of Haitians who were being held without a trial. The AOJ trained hundreds of Haitian judges. Despite these efforts, Haiti's justice system still needs to be modernized and improved.

Law Enforcement

In most countries, including the United States and Canada, the military and the police are two separate groups. The military protects the nation. Police departments operate on a local level, serving cities and towns. Many times during Haiti's history the roles of the military and police have been combined. The military enforced laws and controlled the judicial system. The leaders of this force were often corrupt, and its soldiers acted violently toward innocent Haitians.

Haiti's National Anthem

"La Dessalinienne" ("The Song of Dessalines"), the national anthem of Haiti, was written in honor of Jean-Jacques Dessalines, Haiti's first ruler after independence. Justin Lhérisson, a writer, lawyer, and teacher, wrote the lyrics, and Nicolas Geffrard composed the music. The anthem was adopted in 1904 to celebrate one hundred years of Haitian independence.

Creole lyrics

Pou Ayiti peyi Zansèt yo
Se pou-n mache men nan lamen
Nan mitan-n pa fèt pou gen trèt
Nou fèt pou-n sèl mèt tèt nou
Annou mache men nan lamen
Pou Ayiti ka vin pi bèl
Annou, annou, met tèt ansanm
Pou Ayiti onon tout Zansèt yo.

French lyrics

Pour le Pays, Pour les ancêtres,
Marchons unis, Marchons unis.
Dans nos rangs point de traîtres!
Du sol soyons seuls maîtres.
Marchons unis, Marchons unis
Pour le Pays, Pour les ancêtres,
Marchons, marchons, marchons unis,
Pour le Pays, Pour les ancêtres.

English translation

For our country,
For our forefathers,
United let us march.
Let there be no traitors in our ranks!
Let us be masters of our soil.
United let us march
For our country,
For our forefathers.

When Jean-Bertrand Aristide returned to power in 1994, he hoped to rebuild a safe and peaceful society. To do this, he wanted to get rid of the military, and in 1995, he eliminated the army entirely. That year, the Haitian National Police (HNP) was formed. Yet by late 1996, more than 600 police officers had been accused of selling drugs and committing other crimes. Judges and lawyers were arrested for criminal activity. Crime continued to rise. In 2008, the United Nations sent about 7,000 soldiers and 1,900 police officers to help reduce violence and crime.

A Struggling Economy

WHEN HAITI WAS SAINT-DOMINGUE, IT WAS ONE OF the most profitable colonies in the world. France's economy depended on the colony's production of coffee, sugarcane, and indigo. Today, Haiti is one of the poorest nations in the Western Hemisphere. The statistics tell the story. The average yearly income is only US$1,200, or roughly three dollars a day. More than two-thirds of the labor force do not have regular jobs, and about 80 percent of the people are considered poor. One percent of Haiti's population owns almost 50 percent of the country's wealth. About 58 percent of the population does not have enough food to eat.

The desperate economic crisis was made even worse by the 2010 earthquake. The cost of the damage is estimated to be as high as US$13.2 billion. Haiti faces a long road to recovery.

Opposite: **Haiti produces about 290,000 metric tons of bananas each year.**

Agriculture

About two-thirds of all Haitians work in agriculture, making it the largest segment of Haiti's economy. Most of the farms are small plots, less than 2 acres (0.8 hectares). There is not

Cabbage is one of the many vegetables grown in Haiti.

much fertile soil in Haiti. The land that is fertile is in danger of washing away because of deforestation. A farmer typically grows corn, bananas, beans, and sweet potatoes. Any food the family does not use is sold at a local market.

Coffee, mangoes, and cacao (the source of cocoa, which is used to make chocolate) are also grown. Much of these crops are exported to other countries. Coffee is the most important crop produced in Haiti. It makes up about 20 percent of Haiti's agricultural exports. Haiti was once the third-leading coffee exporter in the world, but production has declined in the last half century. Poor soil quality, outdated production methods, and the absence of trees to protect the crop from direct sunlight are the main reasons for the drop in output.

The production of sugar has also fallen. Until the mid-1980s, sugar was the second most important crop, after coffee. In 1986, the owners of Haiti's leading sugar exporters closed down their operations. They believed more money could be made by importing foreign sugar, rather than exporting what they grew. Today, sugarcane is grown mostly on small farms for personal and local use.

The fishing industry in Haiti is undeveloped because of the lack of money for modern fishing boats and equipment. In recent years, many people have fished part-time because

Haiti's Currency

The gourde is the official currency of Haiti. One gourde is divided into 100 centimes. Paper bills come in values of 10, 20, 25, 50, 100, 250, 500, and 1,000 gourdes. Gourde notes of 1, 2, and 5 are no longer made, although some remain in circulation. Coins have values of 50 centimes, 1 gourde, and 5 gourdes. In 2011, 41 gourdes was worth US$1, and 1 gourde was worth 2 U.S. cents.

Illustrations of famous people and places in history appear on Haiti's money. The 50-gourde note shows Louis Lysius Félicité Salomon Jeune, Haiti's president from 1879 to 1888. Salomon established Haiti's first postal, telegraph, and rural school systems. On the back of the note is the coat of arms of Haiti. The 10-gourde note (right) depicts Sanite Bélair, a heroic woman. She and her husband were executed by the French in 1802 for fighting the army sent by Napoléon. An illustration of Fort Cap Rouge in Jacmel appears on the back of the note.

unemployment is so high. Although the reefs and coastal waters hold fewer fish because of overfishing, fish are still an important part of Haitians' diet.

Mining and Industry

Mining played an important role in Haiti's economy in the 1960s and 1970s. During that time, a U.S. company mined large quantities of copper and bauxite, which is used to make aluminum. Today, stone and sand are mined for use in road and building construction. Despite Haiti's need for new energy sources, none have yet been found. Attempts to uncover oil and lignite, a type of coal, have been unproductive.

Haitians catch fish, conch, and other seafood in the offshore waters.

What Haiti Grows, Makes, and Mines

Agriculture (2007)

Sugarcane	1,000,000 metric tons
Cassava	330,000 metric tons
Bananas	293,000 metric tons

Manufacturing (export value, 2010)

Clothing	US$191,620,000
Essential oils	US$4,960,000

Mining (2007)

Sand	2,000,000 cubic meters

Only 9 percent of Haitians work in industry. The largest source of jobs is in assembly (putting things together). In the 1970s, about 150 foreign companies set up businesses in and around Port-au-Prince. Haitians were employed to make clothing and assemble electronic items and toys. By 1994, all the factories stopped production because of the political instability in the country. Recently, thousands of textile assembly jobs have been created.

Tourism

In the 1950s, Haiti was one of the top tourist spots in the Caribbean. The country's beautiful beaches and sunny skies attracted visitors from many places, especially the United States. During the dictatorship of the Duvaliers, tourism dropped off, but visitors started returning in the 1970s. Cap-Haïtien and Port-au-Prince became popular stopovers for cruise ships. In the 1990s, political turmoil once again kept the visitors away, but the industry is currently recovering. The port of Labadee in the north is a popular resort established by a cruise ship company. Passengers spend a day there but do not visit the rest of Haiti.

A woman buys crafts in Labadee, a popular tourist resort. In other parts of the country, damage caused by the 2010 earthquake and political violence have hurt the tourist industry.

Weights and Measures

Haiti uses the metric system of weights and measures for official purposes. In this system, the basic unit of length is the meter: 1 meter is equal to 39.4 inches, or 3.3 feet. The basic unit of weight is the kilogram: 1 kilogram, or kilo, is equal to 2.2 pounds.

Service Industries

About 25 percent of Haitians work in service industries. These include traders, teachers, gardeners, and many others. Many people run small businesses making furniture, repairing equipment, mending clothes, or breaking rocks for road and building construction. In the capital city of Port-au-Prince, the streets are crowded with people selling fruit and vegetables, soap, used clothing, and other items.

The streets in Port-au-Prince are often crowded with cars.

Transportation

Haiti has an average of twelve motor vehicles for every one thousand people living there. In comparison, the Dominican Republic has sixty-two motor vehicles for each one thousand people. But owning a vehicle can be just as troublesome as not owning one. Roughly 25 percent of Haiti's roads are unpaved. Those that are paved are not well maintained. Mudslides and potholes make travel on many roads difficult if not impossible. In 2004, only 5 percent of the country's roads were in good condition. With the aid of international banks and foreign companies, Haiti began rebuilding its roadways in 2008. More than one hundred projects employing ten thousand people began the job of building a better transport system.

Haiti has fourteen airports, but only four have paved runways. The largest airport, Toussaint Louverture International, once known as Port-au-Prince International, handles most of the country's international flights.

Haiti no longer has a national railway system. The two systems that operated were shut down by 1982. The remaining lines are now used only for transporting sugarcane.

In rural areas, most people travel on *taptaps*, colorful public

Passengers sometimes sit atop crowded, brightly colored taptaps.

Jean-Pierre Boyer ruled Haiti until 1843.

buses. These vehicles are old Japanese-made trucks or vans painted with images of animals, flowers, and other colorful designs. In Port-au-Prince, people often ride in shared taxis called *publiques*. Publiques display a red ribbon on the rearview mirror or radiator cap so that they can be easily identified.

Embargoes and Foreign Aid

The beginnings of Haiti's current financial woes date back to the early years of the newly created republic. In 1820, Jean-Pierre Boyer unified the northern and southern portions of the nation. He needed the other countries of the world to recognize Haiti's independence so that it could trade with them as an equal partner. In 1825, France agreed to recognize Haiti—if Haiti paid France 150 million francs for its losses since Haiti's independence. (It is hard to determine how much this is in today's money, but many historians put it at US$21 billion.) Haiti's history of foreign debt had begun.

For many years, Haiti has received billions of dollars in foreign aid from banks and individual nations. The aid has usually been in the form of loans that Haiti must repay. The biggest bank lenders have been the World Bank, the International Monetary Fund (IMF), and the Inter-American Development Bank (IDB). The United States, Canada, and western European nations have also provided large amounts of aid.

Growing Mangoes

Mangoes are Haiti's second-biggest export crop after coffee. In 2009, Haiti exported US$10 million worth of mangoes, which was one-third of all Haitian agricultural export revenue. Haiti is home to about twenty-five thousand mango farmers and ten million mango trees. There are more than 140 varieties of mangoes, but the Madame Francis is the only one that is exported fresh. Mangoes are grown on the plains and on mountain slopes up to 0.25 miles (400 m) high. They are picked and then transported by animal to local markets. Mangoes grown for export are sold to middlemen who sell them to larger exporting companies. Mangoes offer hope to Haiti's weak economy. It is estimated that mangoes can become a US$90-million-a-year export business.

Haiti is the poorest nation in the Western Hemisphere. People build homes out of whatever materials they can find.

Haiti received much foreign aid during the years that the Duvaliers ruled the nation (1957–1986). The dictators stole hundreds of millions of dollars of this money. Very little of it was used for projects to help Haitians. When Jean-Bertrand Aristide was forced out of office in 1991, other nations in the Western Hemisphere put a trade embargo on Haiti. This means they would not trade with Haiti. The embargo led to fuel and food shortages, increased food prices, and a loss of jobs. Many nations also halted their foreign aid at that time. Aid was resumed after Aristide returned to power in 1994, but tremendous damage had been done to the economy. International aid was again stopped for a time in 2001, when accusations were made that the 2000 presidential election had been unfair.

Hope for the Future?

In 2009, President Préval proposed a plan called the Presidential Commission on Competitiveness to help improve Haiti's productivity and create jobs. The plan called for building up three industries: agriculture, clothing manufacturing, and tourism. Slowly, these industries are growing.

Haiti has also increased its exportation of mangoes and avocados in recent years. Newer crops such as onions, spices, and hot peppers also offer potential as important export foods.

Despite these signs of hope, Haiti faces tremendous economic challenges. Success will depend on creating jobs, improving the environment, and providing basic services, such as health care and sanitation.

In 2008, Haiti produced 325,000 tons (295,000 metric tons) of mangoes and guavas.

The People
of Haiti

84

T HE ORIGINAL INHABITANTS OF HAITI WERE THE TAINO Arawak people. They had been living in the Caribbean for about six hundred years before Europeans came to the Western Hemisphere. When Christopher Columbus arrived in Hispaniola in 1492, about five hundred thousand Tainos lived peacefully on the island. They farmed and hunted, making the most of the island's natural resources.

By about 1550, fewer than five thousand Tainos were still alive. Some had died because the Spanish overworked them. Many others died from diseases the Spanish carried with them. These diseases, such as smallpox and measles, seldom killed Europeans, who had long lived with them. But the Tainos had never before been exposed to them and their bodies could not fight them off.

The Spaniards began bringing enslaved people from Africa to Hispaniola in 1503 to work the fields. Under the French, about six hundred thousand Africans were brought to Haiti to work as slaves on plantations.

Opposite: **Haiti is a young country. In 2011, about 36 percent of the population was under age fifteen.**

The People of Haiti **85**

Today, 95 percent of Haiti's population of 9.7 million are black descendants of the slaves. The rest of the population is white and mulatto. They hold most of the power and wealth in the country.

Mulattoes and Blacks

After the breakup of the colonial plantation system following the Haitian Revolution, mulattoes established their influence in other areas. From the nineteenth century to the present, mulattoes have generally controlled government affairs and professions such as education, medicine, and law. After independence, mulattoes avoided agriculture and local business as ways to earn a living, because they considered them low-class activities. They tended to work and live in Haiti's cities, rather

Arab Haitians

Arabs make up a small but influential portion of Haiti's population. The first group of Arabs to arrive in Haiti came from Syria in 1890. Newly arrived Arabs sold textiles and opened small businesses. During World War I, large numbers of Lebanese immigrated to Haiti. Today, about fifteen thousand people of Lebanese heritage live in the country. Other Arab Haitians came from Palestine and Yemen. Many Arab Haitians have become successful businesspeople, especially in the export and import industries.

Antoine Izméry was a successful Haitian businessman of Palestinian heritage. Izméry supported Jean-Bertrand Aristide in the 1990 presidential election. When Aristide was forced from power in 1991, Izméry began an organization to investigate the overthrow and bring back Aristide's democratic government. In 1993, Izméry was murdered by an antidemocratic military group in Port-au-Prince. The leaders of the group that murdered him were caught but never punished.

Other noted Haitians of Arab ancestry include poet and playwright Nathalie Handal and Samir Mourra, a businessman and candidate in the 2006 Haitian presidential election.

than in the countryside. Wealthy families sent their children to college in Europe.

Blacks make up most of Haiti's lower classes. Conflict between Haiti's poorer blacks and wealthier mulattoes has existed for more than two hundred years.

Common Creole Words and Phrases

Bon jour	Good morning
Mesi	Thank you
Konben?	How much?
Tan pri	Please
Kijan ou rele?	What's your name?
Bonne journee	Have a nice day
Bonswa	Good evening
Mwen pale kreyòl	I speak Haitian Creole

Language

For many years after the revolution, French was Haiti's only official language. It was used in government and business affairs by whites and upper-class mulattoes. Most of the population did not understand it. Instead, they spoke the Creole language, which wealthier people scorned. So, in addition to

Most Haitians speak Creole at home. Some learn French in school.

differences in skin color, the use of two languages also divided the nation.

Today, Haiti has two national languages. In 1987, the new constitution made Creole an official language. Today, almost all Haitians speak Creole, but only about 10 percent of the population speaks French. French is considered a sign of education and wealth. Upper-class Haitians prefer to speak it all the time. The middle class also tries to speak French as often as possible because they consider Creole the language of the lower classes.

Creole began as a language enslaved people used to communicate with the French plantation owners. It is made up of French, African, and Spanish words.

Today, elementary school instruction is in Creole, and French is taught as a second language. High school classes are

Comparing Hispaniola's Health Issues

Haiti and the Dominican Republic both occupy the island of Hispaniola. Here's how they compare on major health issues:

	Haiti	Dominican Republic
Total population	9.7 million	9.8 million
Life expectancy at birth (2006)		
Male	61 years	75 years
Female	63 years	80 years
Deaths under 5 years of age per 1,000 births (2006)	80	29
Estimated number of people with HIV/AIDS (2007)	120,000	57,000
Estimated number of new cases of tuberculosis annually (2007)	29,000	6,800
Amount spent on health care per person (2006)	US$96	US$449

taught in French. But only about 20 percent of Haitian children complete elementary school, so they usually don't learn the French language.

Health

Health care is a serious problem in Haiti. Most people do not have running water in their homes. Only 50 percent of people living in the countryside and 33 percent of people living in cities have any access to clean water. Sewer systems are almost totally absent.

These conditions put Haitians at high risk for disease. Contact with polluted water that contains germs is the cause of diseases such as hepatitis and typhoid. Children are particularly at risk. Of the few hospitals and health

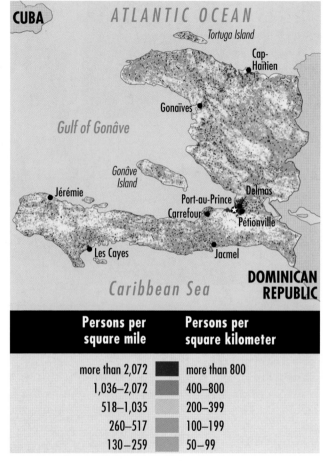

Persons per square mile		Persons per square kilometer
more than 2,072		more than 800
1,036–2,072		400–800
518–1,035		200–399
260–517		100–199
130–259		50–99

Women getting drinking water from a well. Many dangerous diseases are spread in dirty water.

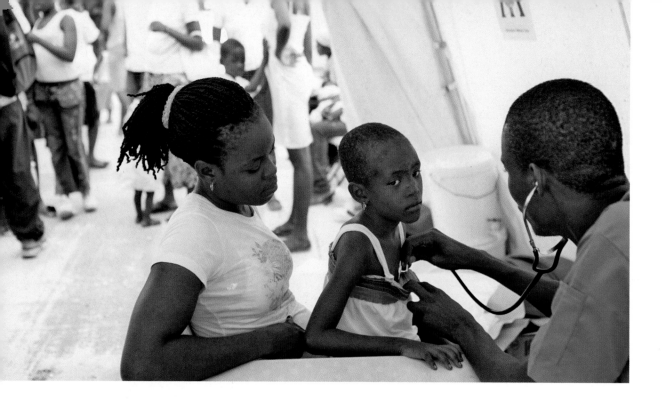

A doctor examines a child in Pétionville. Many Haitians do not have access to medical care.

clinics that there are, many offer poor health care. In 2006, there were only twenty-five doctors and eleven nurses for every one hundred thousand people living in Haiti.

Poverty and Violence

About 80 percent of Haiti's population is poor. Most of these people are farmers who can barely earn a living. The plots of land they farm are often too small to grow enough to feed their families. Erosion of the soil and lack of water make growing crops even more difficult. Some Haitians are so poor that they eat cookies made of dirt or mud. The cookies are usually made with clay, salt, and butter or oil.

In 2008, prices of staples such as rice, beans, corn, and gasoline shot up around the world. Haitians who couldn't afford the increases staged demonstrations in cities around the

Child Slaves

In 2002, a report by the United Nations Children's Fund (UNICEF) claimed that young Haitian children and teens were being sold into the Dominican Republic as slaves. The report proved to be true. Smugglers travel hundreds of miles through both countries picking up and selling children. Most of the children are kidnapped. Others are talked into leaving their poor towns for a chance to earn money. Reports claim that soldiers, border patrols, and government officials are aware of the crime, but do little to stop it.

In 2009, about 950 children were smuggled out of Haiti. In the nine-month period after the January 2010 earthquake, about 7,300 Haitian children were sold into slavery. Many organizations have condemned the activity. They are urging Haiti and the Dominican Republic to work with the United Nations to bring back the children and punish those responsible for the crime.

Haiti also has a tradition known as the *restavek*,

a word that means "stay with." A restavek is a child from a poor country family whose parents send him or her to the city to stay with wealthier acquaintances. The parents hope the child will be sent to school and have a better life in the city. But many times, the host families make the restavek work long hours doing housework and do not send the child to school.

country. The peaceful demonstrations soon turned into "food riots." Some people took to the streets, hurling rocks, smashing windows, and setting fire to cars. Five people were killed, and dozens were injured. Prime Minister Jacques Édouard Alexis was voted out of office by a group of senators for his failure to stop the riots. After a week, President Préval cut the price of rice in the country, convincing the demonstrators to end their protest.

A quick fix to such a serious problem will not have long-lasting results. Only years of planning, funding, and the hard work of all Haitians will turn things around.

Spiritual Life

F OR HUNDREDS OF YEARS, ROMAN CATHOLICISM WAS THE only official religion of Haiti. It had been brought to the island by the Spanish and was later practiced by the French. Enslaved people shipped to Haiti had brought their own African religious beliefs and practices. Many slaves merged their African traditions with Roman Catholicism, and by the early 1800s, a new religion called Vodou was born. In 2003, Vodou was recognized as an official religion of Haiti. Although most Haitians are Roman Catholic, many also practice Vodou.

Opposite: **Some Haitians dress up to celebrate All Souls' Day, which is also called the Day of the Dead.**

Roman Catholicism

Only upper- and middle-class mulattoes observe Catholicism as their sole religion. They believe it is a symbol of the French culture, so they want to remain connected to it. To them, Vodou is a religion practiced only by the poor and uneducated.

During the twentieth century, the Catholic Church's attitude toward Vodou began to change. After attempting to rid the nation of Vodou, the church began programs of educating the poor, rather than trying to stop them from practicing their

Haiti's Religions

Roman Catholic	80%
Protestant	16%
Other	3%
None	1%

Note: Approximately half the population practices Vodou in addition to another religion.

Catholicism has been the main religion in Haiti since Europeans first arrived in the region five hundred years ago. Today, four out of every five Haitians are Catholic.

religion. Church leaders supported the new constitution of 1987, even though it allowed the practice of Vodou.

The Catholic Church remains a strong force in Haiti's daily life, and Haitian life has an effect on the church. Drummers beat rhythms at services, and Mass is sung in Creole. The church has often spoken out against Haiti's dictatorships, especially against Duvalier. The church supported the prodemocracy Jean-Bertrand Aristide, a former Catholic priest, each time he ran for president.

Vodou

Vodou has no central church or text. It is a system of beliefs that Haitians celebrate in dance, song, and prayer. The faith is based on *lwas*, which are spirits that communicate with humans. Each lwa is different, and some say there are as many as two hundred of them. Each lwa has his or her own personality, way of dressing, and way of speaking. Each responds to different songs, dances, and rhythms. Lwas allow people to interact with Bondye, the most supreme and distant god. Inside the physical body of every human being is a *gro-bon-ange* ("big good angel") and a *ti-bon-ange* ("little good angel"). The gro-bon-ange is a person's soul. The ti-bon-ange is the conscience, or the part that is able to tell right from wrong.

People bathe in a muddy pool as part of a Vodou ritual.

A mambo (in purple) offers a candle to a lwa.

When a person dies, the gro-bon-ange becomes a lwa. Two popular lwas are Ezili Freda Daome and Gede. Ezili Freda Daome represents love and beauty. Her symbol is a heart. Gede is the lord of the dead and guards graveyards, where he keeps the dead souls in and the live souls out.

A minister, called a *houngan* (if male) or *mambo* (if female) leads each group of Vodou practitioners. Ceremonies are held for different reasons, usually to ask for the blessing of a lwa or to communicate with the spirit of a dead relative. In a typical ceremony, the people gather around a pole in the middle of a large room. Lwas are then called upon with a sacred rattle

A Dictionary of Vodou Terms

baka   An evil spirit that can assume various animal forms

Erzuli   The beautiful female lwa of love and compassion

lwa   The spirits or mysteries of Vodou

wanga   Objects that have magically been given a property that can be harmful to humans

zombi   A dead human who comes back to life without a soul and is then under the control of a magician

(*ason*) and the beating of drums. The lwa comes down the pole and takes possession of one of the people, usually the houngan. The lwa communicates to the group through the priest. During the ceremony, people sing and dance while they are in trances.

Dancing is an important part of the Vodou religion.

Animal sacrifice is part of Vodou. Here, a mambo holds the head of a bull that was killed during a ceremony.

Animal sacrifices are often part of the Vodou ceremony. It is thought that lwas must be fed to maintain their energies, which keep the world in harmony. Goats, pigs, and chickens are typically sacrificed and then cooked and fed to the ceremony's participants.

Vodou worshippers see no conflict between their religion and Christianity. They believe in one god and in the Christian Jesus. But they also believe that God does not intervene in daily human affairs; instead that is the realm of the lwas.

Haiti's Religious Holidays

Carnival	Late January into February
Holy Thursday	March or April
Good Friday	March or April
Easter Sunday	March or April
Assumption Day	August 15
All Saints' Day	November 1
All Souls' Day	November 2
Christmas	December 25

Protestants

The first Protestants to arrive in Haiti were missionaries in the mid-1800s. Their goal was to convert Haitians from Catholicism and Vodou. Today, about 16 percent of Haitians are Protestants. The largest group is Baptists, who make up

A group of Baptists worship at a small church in the Central Plateau.

Evangelical Protestants try to convince others to join their faith. Here, an Evangelical group holds a procession near Port-au-Prince.

about 10 percent, while Pentecostals make up 4 percent. Other Protestant groups in Haiti include Methodists, Episcopalians, Jehovah's Witnesses, Mormons, and Presbyterians. In the 1970s, Evangelical Protestant missionaries began coming to Haiti in large numbers. They are strongly opposed to Vodou, claiming it is devil worship.

An estimated four thousand to five thousand Muslims live in Haiti today. Muslims have a long history in Haiti. Some enslaved Africans brought to Haiti hundreds of years ago were Muslim, although most were forced to stop practicing their religion. A large number of Arab immigrants came to Haiti in the early twentieth century, which reestablished Islam in the country. Most Haitian Muslims live in Port-au-Prince.

There are fewer than fifty Jews currently living in Haiti. During World War II, Jewish people were persecuted in Germany and other parts of Europe. Haiti opened its doors to a limited number of European immigrants, and about three hundred Jews fled there to avoid persecution. In recent years, many Jews have left Haiti because of the poor economy and violence. Most have gone to the United States or Panama.

The Ti Legliz Movement

While he was studying to be a priest in the 1960s, Jean-Bertrand Aristide became influenced by liberation theology, which said the church should work for social and economic justice for everyone. Liberation theology argued that all people had the right to be free and live with dignity. When the idea took hold in Haiti, it became known as Ti Legliz, Creole for "Little Church." Aristide became one of the most important people in the movement.

In the 1970s, people began using churches not only for prayer meetings but also as adult learning centers and places to discuss politics and social issues. Haitian priests and nuns called for the end of government and upper-class injustices against the poor. Church officials taught people to read, gave them clothing, and established health clinics.

Haitians were encouraged by the positive change that the Ti Legliz groups, numbering in the thousands, could bring to their lives. The movement quickly grew, especially in the countryside and among poor youth in the city slums. Many people believe it was responsible for finally overthrowing the corrupt Duvalier regime.

A Bountiful Culture

D ESPITE ITS POLITICAL AND ECONOMIC TROUBLES, Haiti's culture, art, and music are a colorful mix of creativity and imagination. By combining the culture of their African roots with French influences, Haitians have developed a style that is unique to their country. Bold, vibrant colors appear on buses, houses, churches, pottery, traditional costumes, and tapestries. Haiti's music is rhythmic and energetic, coming alive in the soulful dancing of the people.

Opposite: **A mural of Toussaint Louverture brightens a wall in Port-au-Prince.**

The Beating of the Drums

Most Haitian dances come from Vodou traditions. The purpose of many dances is to ask the lwas for protection and inspiration. Dancing is also done to celebrate holidays or festivals, or express thanks for a good harvest of the crops. Dancing for pleasure is called *pou paisi*. One of the most popular dances of this kind is the up-tempo merengue. Partners hold each other closely and swing their hips in rhythm while doing graceful twists and turns together.

Rara dancers take to the streets in wild costumes during Carnival.

During the holiday of Carnival, which begins in January, masked dancers called *rara* dance in the streets in wildly colorful costumes. Musicians who play bamboo trumpets called *vaccines* usually appear with the rara dancers.

Kompa is a popular form of Haitian music that is played at social dances called *bambouches*. It is a slowed-down version of merengue music and is an easy dance to learn. Kompa bands use guitar, keyboard, and Vodou drumming in their performances. Roots, or Vodou music, developed in the 1980s as a form of protest music. The song lyrics often call for social change. Roots music has become popular throughout the world.

Drums are the heart and soul of all Haitian music. The *rada* is a set of three drums used in Vodou ceremonies. The largest drum in a rada is the *mama*, which is played with a wooden hammer. The *seconde* drum is struck with a *baguette*, a piece of wood with a cord. The *boula* is the smallest drum and is hit with two sticks. There are three types of drums played during Carnival. The largest is about 3 feet tall (1 m) and is shaped like an ice cream cone. Another type of drum is hung around the musician's neck, and is played by hand. There is also a double-headed drum that the player beats with his hands or with sticks.

Drumming is central to Haitian music.

After the Funeral

In Haiti, when a parent dies, the family is responsible for feeding the nearby community every night for nine days. The family also builds a small house made of concrete and bricks in the cemetery. The deceased is laid to rest in the house. To raise money for these practices, poor families have to sell off parts of their farms. As Haiti endures economic decline, these practices are harder for poor families to afford.

Literature

Over the last one hundred years, Haitian literature has often focused on national pride and human rights. In the 1930s and 1940s, writers such as Jean Price-Mars, Leon Laleau, and Jacques Roumain wrote about their African heritage, Haitian poverty, and Haiti's struggle against colonial powers. Price-Mars was a defender of Vodou and an outspoken opponent of the U.S. occupation of Haiti between 1915 and 1934. In his 1928 novel, *Ainsi Parla l'Oncle* (*Thus Spoke the Uncle*), Price-Mars wrote about Haiti's poor black farmers and urged wealthy Haitians to take pride in their country's rich African culture. Laleau was appointed to several government positions but is best known for his writings, which expressed the sadness and character of Haiti's people. Roumain's *Gouverneurs de la Rosée* (*Masters of the Dew*) explored the frustration and anger of Haitians through the eyes of people living in a poor country village.

Edwidge Danticat moved to New York City at age twelve, but she remains deeply connected to her homeland. Most of her stories and essays concern Haitian life and history.

In more recent years, René Depestre's novel *The Festival of the Greasy Pole* told about the horrors of the Duvalier regime and the influence of Vodou on everyday life in Haiti. Edwidge Danticat is an award-winning writer of novels, short stories, and movie documentaries. In her best-selling 1994 novel, *Breath, Eyes, Memory*, she wrote about Creole life, Vodou culture, and the horrors of the Tontons Macoutes.

Voice of the People

Félix Morisseau-Leroy was a poet and playwright, and one of Haiti's most popular heroes. He was the first important writer to work in the Creole language. His plays, poems, and articles helped make Creole an accepted language in Haiti's schools. "Moriso," as he was nicknamed, gave millions of Haitians around the world a sense of pride in their Creole language and united them in appreciation of their Haitian heritage. His work eventually led to Creole becoming recognized as an official language of Haiti in 1961.

Morisseau-Leroy, the son of wealthy mulattoes, was born near Jacmel. He studied at Columbia University in New York City and then returned to Haiti, where he taught in Port-au-Prince. His first major work was his Creole version of the classic Greek play *Antigone*, published in 1953. He set his version of the play in a Haitian village. The main character was a powerful Vodou priest.

For the first time, Haitians saw how complex and powerful their language could be in a dramatic performance.

In 1959, Morisseau-Leroy fled Haiti when François Duvalier became president. Duvalier thought Morisseau-Leroy's writing was a danger to his dictatorship. Morisseau-Leroy continued to write and teach in France, Nigeria, Ghana, and Senegal. By 1981, he had moved to Miami, Florida, where the large Haitian community treated him as a hero. He returned briefly to Haiti in 1986, when Jean-Claude Duvalier was exiled. In 1991, he attended the inauguration of Jean-Bertrand Aristide as a guest speaker.

One of his most important works was a novel called *Les Djons d'Haiti Tom (People of Haiti with Courage)*. It tells the story of the people of Jacmel from the time of the U.S. invasion in 1915 to the overthrow of President Aristide in 1991.

Art

Haitian artists express their boundless creativity in countless forms that include paintings, sculpture, crafts, murals, and sequined flags used in Vodou ceremonies. In the mid-1940s, American teacher DeWitt Peters and Haitian artist Albert Mangones established the Centre d'Art in Port-au-Prince to encourage Haitian artists. Many of the artists used a simple style, called primitive, or naïve, art. Philomé Obin is called the father of the primitive movement, but Hector Hyppolite is probably the movement's most famous painter. Hyppolite was a Vodou priest who earned money by painting windows, doors, and buildings.

Georges Liautaud was a blacksmith who worked with the center in the early 1950s, making decorative metal sculptures. His work led to a style in which artists cut old metal oil drums into unusual sculptures.

A market scene painted on a wall in Port-au-Prince. Haitian art often uses bright colors.

Drapo

In the 1980s and 1990s, artists in the Bel Air district began making *drapo*, or sequined flags, that showed various Vodou lwas. The colorful, sparkling flags are used in ceremonies to call on the spirits to help priests and practitioners communicate with the lwas. Most drapo are about 2 to 3 square feet (0.2 to 0.3 sq m) and require fifteen thousand to forty thousand individual sequins to make.

Many Haitian artists work in unusual forms. Jerry Rosembert (right) makes paintings on walls all over Port-au-Prince.

A member of the Haitian national soccer team (in blue and red) fights for the ball in a match against Brazil.

Sports

Soccer is Haiti's most popular sport. Both men and women play it professionally. The Fédération Haïtienne de Football is in charge of the Haitian national team. About thirty officials from the federation were killed during the 2010 earthquake. The national soccer arena, the Sylvio Cator Stadium in Port-au-Prince, suffered tremendous damage. Tents were set up on the artificial turf for people left homeless by the disaster. People bathed on the sidelines and cooked in the dugouts.

In October 2010, the International Olympic Committee (IOC) announced that it would build a new sports center in Haiti. The new center will probably contain indoor and outdoor tracks, fields, classrooms, and a library.

Some people in Haiti play basketball and tennis. These sports are less common than soccer, however, because they require special equipment and locations that most Haitians cannot afford.

Teenagers play basketball at a camp set up for people who lost their homes in the earthquake in 2010.

The Haitian Who Vanished

On the evening of June 29, 1950, at Independence Stadium in Belo Horizonte, Brazil, the U.S. soccer team shocked the sports world by upsetting England in a World Cup match. The hero of the game was Joe Gaetjens (above right), a Haitian-born player, who scored the only goal in the historic contest.

Gaetjens was born in Port-au-Prince in 1924. In 1947, he went to New York City, where he studied accounting. He soon started playing soccer for a local team and was invited at the last minute to join the U.S. soccer squad for the World Cup play-offs in Brazil. After scoring his famous goal, Gaetjens went to France and played soccer.

When he returned to Port-au-Prince in 1953, a huge crowd was there to greet him. They carried a banner reading THE BEST PLAYER IN HAITI, THE USA AND THE WORLD. Haitians had not forgotten Gaetjens—he was their national hero.

When François Duvalier was elected president in 1957, he took revenge on his opponents. Gaetjens's family had supported Duvalier's rival candidate, Louis Déjoie, in the elections. Duvalier wanted to get rid of the entire Gaetjens family. On July 8, 1964, two thugs jumped into the car Joe was driving, pulled out guns, and drove away with him. He was thrown in a Tontons Macoute police wagon and never heard from again.

After eight years, the Haitian government admitted that Gaetjens had died. Some people claimed he was shot by guards. Others said he died in prison. To this day, no one knows exactly what happened to Joe Gaetjens.

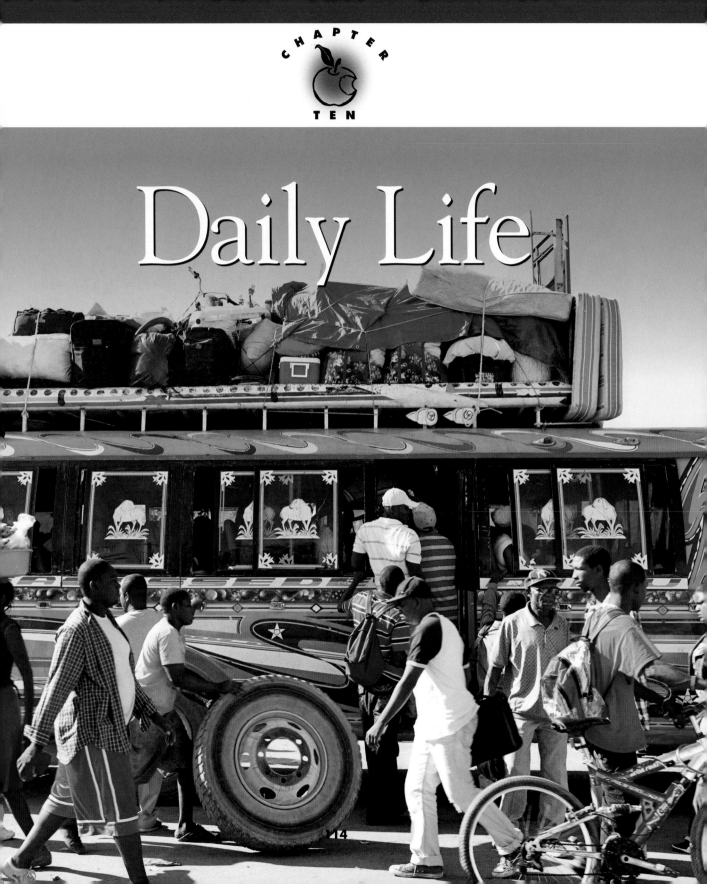

Daily Life

THE COLORFULLY PAINTED TAPTAP BUSES, WHICH TRAVEL
the streets of Haiti's cities, often have inspirational slogans on
them. After the 2010 earthquake, one of the buses carried a
sign that read, LIFE IS NOT ONLY ROSES—IT IS SOMETIMES DARK.
For most Haitians, daily life is *often* dark. Poverty, unemployment, hunger, and crime are constant challenges for most of
the population. Yet Haitians believe their spirit and strength
will lead them to better times ahead.

Opposite: **Brightly colored taptaps are part of everyday life in Haiti.**

Education

Public education in Haiti is free, but books and other materials
must be paid for. Children in poor areas usually cannot afford
to go to school. Throughout the country, there is a shortage
of school supplies and qualified teachers. Only 20 percent of
elementary school teachers are trained.

Children begin kindergarten when they are three or four
years old. Then they attend elementary school for another six
years. It is estimated that about two-thirds of Haiti's children
complete their primary-school education.

All Haitian children wear uniforms to school.

Few poor children attend a public secondary school. There is only a small number of schools, and they are spread over long distances. Getting to and from school often requires miles of walking. The quality of secondary education is poor. Schools are overcrowded and badly managed. Most public high schools have no libraries. Many times the teacher has the only textbook in the class. The high school program lasts seven years, but most students drop out before they complete their studies. Students can also attend vocational schools where they learn a trade, such as a technical job in industry. About 25 percent of high school students attend vocational schools. These schools are usually poorly maintained and have little or no equipment.

Several new government programs to improve public education give hope to Haiti's children. One program plans to train 2,400 new teachers every year, instead of the 400 teachers who are currently trained each year. Another plan is to give more children access to public preschool programs. The success of plans such as these depends largely on a stable Haitian government and continued financial support by banks and countries around the world.

Only about 20 percent of children in Haiti go to secondary school.

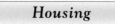
Housing for poor Haitians, in the cities or in the countryside, is very simple. City dwellers with jobs often rent a couple of rooms for their family. The houses are usually made of cinder blocks and have tin roofs. The unemployed live in shacks made of wood, tin, or cardboard. There is usually no electricity or running water.

In rural areas, houses are often built with strips of wood covered with clay. The roofs are made of straw or tin. The floors of the houses are densely packed earth.

Many people in Haiti live in simple shacks, often made of tin and cardboard.

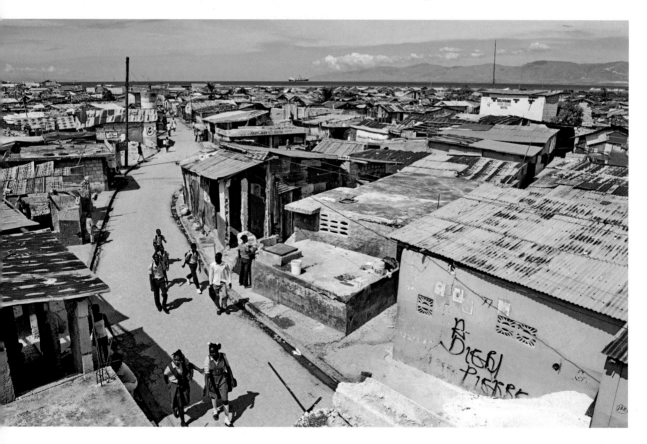

In Haiti, cars are supposed to drive on the right side of the road, but few roads have lines painted on them. Drivers use whatever side of the road is open. There are few road signs, and accurate maps are generally unavailable. The roads are poorly maintained and are often filled with potholes. The government has few resources to help drivers in trouble or to clear the road of accidents or broken-down vehicles that are blocking traffic. Day or night, driving in Haiti can be a dangerous adventure.

Wealthier people in cities such as Port-au-Prince sometimes live in elaborate mansions, decorated with fancy ironwork and woodwork. Usually painted a sparkling white, these homes have running water, electricity, and modern appliances.

Shantytowns

Shantytowns exist in most urban areas in Haiti. They are built when poor farmers and their families move to the city to find a better life. Without money, they have to make their own houses, often of plywood, sheets of metal and plastic, and just about anything they can find. There is usually no electricity, running water, sewers, or government services of any kind. Crime and violence, drug use, and disease are all problems in the shantytowns.

One of the worst shantytowns in the world is Cité Soleil in Port-au-Prince. More than three hundred thousand people, living in extreme poverty, are packed into the slum. An estimated 60 to 70 percent of these people do not have access to even the most basic bathroom facilities. Crime is common, and the Haitian police are reluctant to enter the area. Most of the people living in Cité Soleil are children or young adults. Ninety percent of them are too poor to go to school. Several international relief organizations are working to improve conditions in the slum, but one resident sadly claims, "There are so many social problems in Cité Soleil that *everyone* here is a victim."

Young women carry water home to Cité Soleil, where there is no running water.

The Red Cross in Cité Soleil

"When you have nothing, you are nobody. You are less than nothing. We want Cité Soleil to change. Change, that's all we ask for." These were the words of a man who lives in the slums of Cité Soleil. Today, the International Committee of the Red Cross (ICRC) is showing that change is possible. In 2004, the ICRC began training first-aid personnel in Cité Soleil to help get people injured in gang warfare to hospitals. In 2005, about seven hundred people were whisked to medical care in local taxis.

The ICRC has also won the cooperation of gangs, who generally do not like outside groups in the shantytown. Gang members think people from the Red Cross might be able to ease the misery in Cité Soleil. Together, the ICRC and local gangs run a water and

sanitation program. The ICRC has even convinced some governmental agencies, such as the water and garbage collection departments, to return to the shantytown. Working with local groups, the ICRC has cleaned out filthy canals and restored about fifty public water spots.

The ICRC cannot eliminate Cité Soleil's terrible problems. Yet as Cedric Piralla, an ICRC official says, "The Red Cross is not going to replace the government. But it can contribute to saving lives. And that's what the first-aiders are doing."

Haitians enjoy fish, which they sometimes catch themselves.

Food

Haitian food has a mix of African, French, and Spanish influences. The basic foods of Haitian cuisine are rice, millet (a kind of grain), corn, and yam. The national dish is rice and beans, or *riz et pois*. Green vegetables and tropical fruits also play a large role in Haiti's diet. Citrus fruits, avocados, and mangoes grow well and are particularly healthy food choices.

Haitians do not eat much meat because it is expensive. Chicken and goat are the most common meats. Haitians enjoy fish and shellfish, but overfishing has made it less common and more expensive to buy.

Creole cooking features many locally grown herbs and spices, especially peppers. *Calalou* is a tasty traditional dish made with pork, crabmeat, spinach, peppers, and onions. It is usually served with rice. *Du riz a legumes* (rice with vegetables) is a hearty stew made with eggplant, spinach, carrots, and beef. A favorite snack food is *banane pésée*, fried slices of plantain, a kind of starchy green banana. Banane pésée is often eaten with goat or pork. A popular sauce used in soups and stews and put on rice and beans is *épis*, made from garlic, peppers, and herbs.

Beans are an important part of the Haitian diet. They are inexpensive and nourishing.

Pain Haïtien

Here's an easy recipe for tasty *pain Haïtien*, or Haitian bread.

Ingredients

2 packages active dry yeast
1½ cups warm water
¼ cup honey
2 tablespoons vegetable oil
1 teaspoon salt
¾ teaspoon ground nutmeg
4 cups flour
¼ teaspoon instant coffee
2 tablespoons milk

Directions

Preheat the oven to 350°F. Dissolve the yeast in a large bowl with the warm water. Stir in the honey, oil, salt, nutmeg, and 2 cups of flour. Beat for about 1 minute, or until the mixture is very smooth.

Slowly add enough of the remaining flour to make a stiff dough. Turn dough onto a lightly floured surface. Knead the dough until it's smooth, about 5 minutes. Place the dough in a greased bowl, cover, and let rise in a warm place until it doubles in size, about 50 minutes. Punch down the dough.

Press the dough into a greased pan (about 15 inches x 10 inches) and cut it into 2½-inch squares (only cut two-thirds of the way through the dough). Cover and let rise until double in size, about 30 minutes. Dissolve the instant coffee in the milk and brush over the dough. Bake until the bread is golden brown, about 35 minutes. Makes about 24 squares.

Like people in any culture, Haitians eat many types of desserts, often sweetened by homegrown sugarcane. A type of Italian ice called *fresco* is made with a heavy fruit syrup. *Akasant*, a thick corn milkshake, is made with evaporated milk, sugar, and corn flour.

Holiday Festivals

Celebrations play an important role in the life of all Haitians. Whether it's a religious holiday or a civic one, festivals are celebrated with costumes and energetic music and dancing.

January 1 is Independence Day, celebrating Haiti's declaration of independence from the French in 1804. It is both a serious and joyous occasion. People place flowers at important buildings and landmarks to remember those who died in Haiti's struggle for freedom. Parades are held in large cities such as Port-au-Prince to celebrate the day. January 2 is called Ancestors' Day, or Heroes' Day. A greased pole is put up in the center of town, and money and pastries are placed on top of the pole. Young men try to climb the pole to reach the treats.

Girls dance around a maypole at an Easter celebration.

Carnival, also called Rara, is one of Haiti's most joyous times of year. It starts in January and usually ends in February or early March, just before the beginning of Lent, a forty-day period leading up to Easter. Rara bands march through the streets singing, dancing, and playing music. In the days before Lent, huge parades with elaborate floats are the main attraction.

Spring Festival begins on May 1, which is Labor Day. It runs for three days and features parades with lots of dancing and feasting. November 2 is All Souls' Day, a time for honoring the dead. People visit cemeteries and place flowers and candles at the graves of their ancestors. Vodou ceremonies take place in many cemeteries. People paint their faces white to mimic the paleness of death. They say prayers to the lwas of the dead, Baron Samedi and Gede.

National Holidays

January 1	Independence Day
January 2	Ancestors' Day
April 14	Pan-American Day
May 1	Labor Day and Agriculture Day
May 18	Flag and University Day
May 22	National Sovereignty Day
October 17	Anniversary of the death of Dessalines
October 24	United Nations Day
November 1	All Saints' Day
November 2	All Souls' Day
November 18	Battle of Vertières Day
December 5	Discovery of Haiti Day
December 25	Christmas Day

A young man with his grand-father. Through the years, Haitians have shown the strength to endure.

Is There Hope?

Before it declared its independence more than two hundred years ago, Haiti was called France's Pearl of the Antilles. But the reality was much darker. It was a place where nine out of ten people lived in slavery. Today, Haiti and its people are free, but the nation remains hobbled by deep economic and political problems. Sometimes it seems as if Haiti's future is hopeless. Yet Haitians have a history of rising to their many challenges and overcoming their difficulties.

No one knows what Haiti's future will be, but if the nation succeeds in pulling itself from the particularly desperate situation created by the 2010 earthquake, it will be the character of the Haitian people that does it. As a writer for the *Miami Herald* said almost twenty years ago, "In a country so lacking in natural wealth and political freedom, kindness and hope are powerful supports. Therein lies the Haitians' capacity for enduring. Haitians are world champions of endurance!"

Timeline

Haitian History		World History
		ca. **2500** BCE Egyptians build the pyramids and the Sphinx in Giza.
		ca. **563** BCE The Buddha is born in India.
		313 CE The Roman emperor Constantine legalizes Christianity.
		610 The Prophet Muhammad begins preaching a new religion called Islam.
The Taino Arawak people begin living in the Caribbean.	ca. **900**	
		1054 The Eastern (Orthodox) and Western (Roman Catholic) Churches break apart.
		1095 The Crusades begin.
		1215 King John seals the Magna Carta.
		1300s The Renaissance begins in Italy.
		1347 The plague sweeps through Europe.
		1453 Ottoman Turks capture Constantinople, conquering the Byzantine Empire.
Europeans first arrive on Hispaniola.	**1492**	**1492** Columbus arrives in North America.
Black Africans are first brought to Hispaniola.	**1503**	**1500s** Reformers break away from the Catholic Church, and Protestantism is born.
The Treaty of Ryswick divides Hispaniola between the French in the west and the Spanish in the east.	**1697**	
Port-au-Prince is founded.	**1749**	
		1776 The U.S. Declaration of Independence is signed.
The Haitian Revolution is launched by black slaves and mulattoes.	**1791**	**1789** The French Revolution begins.
Slavery is abolished in all French colonies.	**1794**	
Haiti achieves independence from France.	**1804**	
Jean-Jacques Dessalines declares himself emperor.	**1805**	
Dessalines is assassinated; Haiti is divided into a black-controlled north and a mulatto-ruled south.	**1806**	

Haitian History

Jean-Pierre Boyer unifies Haiti.	1820
Haiti gains control of Santo Domingo (present-day Dominican Republic).	1822
The military overthrows Boyer.	1843
The Dominican Republic becomes independent from Haiti.	1844
The United States invades Haiti.	1915
U.S. troops withdraw from Haiti.	1934
François "Papa Doc" Duvalier becomes president of Haiti.	1957
Papa Doc dies; his son, Jean-Claude "Baby Doc" Duvalier, assumes control.	1971
Jean-Claude Duvalier flees Haiti.	1986
Jean-Bertrand Aristide becomes president but is soon overthrown by the military.	1991
The military government is forced out; Aristide returns to power.	1994
Aristide is reelected president.	2000
Aristide is forced into exile.	2004
René Préval is elected president.	2006
In January, a magnitude 7.0 earthquake shakes Port-au-Prince, killing about 316,000 people.	2010

World History

1865	The American Civil War ends.
1879	The first practical lightbulb is invented.
1914	World War I begins.
1917	The Bolshevik Revolution brings communism to Russia.
1929	A worldwide economic depression begins.
1939	World War II begins.
1945	World War II ends.
1957	The Vietnam War begins.
1969	Humans land on the Moon.
1975	The Vietnam War ends.
1989	The Berlin Wall is torn down as communism crumbles in Eastern Europe.
1991	The Soviet Union breaks into separate states.
2001	Terrorists attack the World Trade Center in New York City and the Pentagon in Washington, D.C.
2004	A tsunami in the Indian Ocean destroys coastlines in Africa, India, and Southeast Asia.
2008	The United States elects its first African American president.

Fast Facts

Official name: Haiti

Capital: Port-au-Prince

Official languages: French and Creole

Port-au-Prince

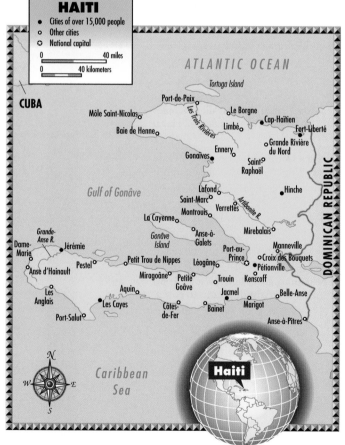

Haitian flag

Official religion: None

Year of founding: 1804

National anthem: "La Dessalinienne" ("The Song of Dessalines")

Government: Republic

Chief of state: President

Head of government: Prime minister

Area: 10,714 square miles (27,749 sq km)

Latitude and longitude: 19° 00' N and 72° 25' W

Bordering country: Dominican Republic to the east

Highest elevation: Pic la Selle, 8,793 feet (2,680 m) above sea level

Lowest elevation: Sea level along the coast

Average temperature: 77°F (25°C) in January; 84°F (29°C) in July

Average precipitation: Varies greatly, from 12 inches (30 cm) in the northwest to 120 inches (305 cm) in the mountainous regions of the southwest

Southern coast

Citadelle Laferrière

Currency

National population: 9,719,932 (2011 est.)

Population of largest cities (2010 est.):

Port-au-Prince	2,350,000
Carrefour	430,250
Delmas	359,451
Pétionville	271,175
Cap-Haïtien	155,505

Famous landmarks:
- ▶ *Citadelle Laferrière,* Milot
- ▶ *Pic Macaya National Park,* Massif de la Hotte
- ▶ *Sans-Souci Palace,* Milot

Economy: Roughly two-thirds of all Haitians work in agriculture, mostly as small-scale farmers. Haiti's chief crops are coffee, mangoes, sugarcane, and rice. Haiti's manufacturing industry employs only 9 percent of the population. Natural resources found in Haiti include bauxite, copper, gold, and marble. Haiti's once-successful tourist industry has been harmed by natural disasters, poverty, and political instability. Foreign aid accounts for roughly 30 to 40 percent of Haiti's national budget.

Currency: The gourde. In March 2011, 41 gourdes equaled US$1.00.

System of weights and measures: Metric system

Literacy rate: 62%

Schoolchildren

Edwidge Danticat

Words and phrases in Haitian Creole:

Kijan ou rele?	What's your name?
Bonswa.	Good evening.
M pral travay.	I'm going to work.
Èske ou konn ale Ayiti?	Have you been to Haiti?
Bonne journee.	Have a nice day.
Atansyon!	Attention!/Watch out!
Mwen pale kreyòl.	I speak Haitian Creole.

Prominent Haitians:

Jean-Bertrand Aristide (1953–)
President

Edwidge Danticat (1969–)
Author

René Depestre (1926–)
Poet

Jean-Jacques Dessalines (1758–1806)
Leader of the slave revolt

Hector Hyppolite (1894–1948)
Artist

Toussaint Louverture (1743–1803)
Rebel leader; governor of Saint-Domingue

To Find Out More

Books

- ▶ Coupeau, Steeve. *The History of Haiti*. Westport, CT: Greenwood Press, 2008.

- ▶ Dash, J. Michael. *Culture and Customs of Haiti*. Westport, CT: Greenwood Press, 2008.

- ▶ Goldstein, Margaret J. *Haiti in Pictures*. Minneapolis, MN: Lerner, 2006.

- ▶ Kallen, Stuart A. *Voodoo*. San Diego: Lucent, 2005.

- ▶ Lies, Anne. *The Earthquake in Haiti*. Edina, MN: Abdo Publishing, 2011.

DVDs

- ▶ *Égalité for All: Toussaint Louverture and the Haitian Revolution*. PBS Home Video, 2010.

- ▶ *Haiti*. 60 Minutes, 2010.

- ▶ *Voodoo and the Church in Haiti*. CustomFlix, 2007.

Web Sites

▶ **BBC News: Haiti country profile**
http://news.bbc.co.uk/2/hi
/americas/country_profiles
/1202772.stm
For an overview of recent history and links to news stories.

▶ **World Factbook**
www.cia.gov/library
/publications/the-world-factbook
/geos/ha.html
For current reports and statistics about Haiti.

▶ **World Health Organization: Haiti**
www.who.int/countries/hti/en
Key statistics and reports on the state of Haiti's health.

Embassies

▶ **Embassy of Haiti**
2311 Massachusetts Ave., NW
Washington, DC 20008
202/332-4090
http://haiti.org

▶ **Embassy of Haiti in Canada**
130 Albert Street, Suite 1409
Ottawa, Ontario K1P 5G4
Canada
613/238-1628

Index

Page numbers in *italics* indicate illustrations.

Meet the Author

NEL YOMTOV IS AN AWARD-WINNING AUTHOR AND EDITOR with a passion for writing nonfiction books for young people. Bitten by the reading bug at an early age, he learned how books could be the doorway to the wonders of our world and its people. Writing gives him an opportunity to investigate the subjects he loves best and to share his discoveries with young readers. In recent years, he has written books about history and geography, as well as graphic-novel adaptations of classic mythology, sports biographies, and science.

Nel Yomtov was born in New York City. After graduating from college, he worked at Marvel Comics, where he handled all phases of comic book production work. By the time he left seven years later, he was supervisor of the product development division of Marvel's licensing program. Yomtov has also written, edited, and colored hundreds of Marvel comic books.

Yomtov has served as editorial director of a children's nonfiction book publisher and as publisher of the Hammond World Atlas book division. In between, he squeezed in a two-year stint as consultant to Major League Baseball, where he helped run an educational program for elementary and middle schools throughout the country.

Yomtov conducted the research for this book about Haiti from libraries in New York, newspapers, magazines, and Web sites. He particularly enjoyed reading *Dignity*, by former Haitian president Jean-Bertrand Aristide. It is an inspirational book about Haiti's fight for democracy and freedom.

Yomtov lives in the New York area with his wife, Nancy, a teacher and writer. His son, Jess, a college student, is a journalism major and a broadcaster for his college radio station. Nel Yomtov can often be found on the softball fields in New York's Central Park or at a local blues club honking on his harmonicas.

Photo Credits

Photographs © 2012:

age fotostock/Louise Murray/Robert Harding Picture Library: back cover;
Alamy Images: 19 (JS Callahan/tropicalpix), 22 (Brendan Hoffman), 105 (Roger Hutchings), 122 (Florian Kopp/imagebroker), 127 (Jake Lyell), 17 (Mediacolor's), 73, 132 bottom (Glyn Thomas);
Animals Animals/Zigmund Leszcynski: 37;
AP Images: 111 (Walter Astrada), 92 (CHESNOT/SIPA), 65 (Ariana Cubillos), 76, 106 (Ariana Cubillos), 60 (Ramon Espinosa), 119 (Andres Leighton), 64 (Daniel Morel), 66 left (Shehzad Noorani/Canadian Press), 107, 133 bottom (Seth Wenig);
Art Resource, NY/Réunion des Musées Nationaux: 12, 45;
Bridgeman Art Library International Ltd., London/New York/Philomé Obin/Private Collection: 50;
Corbis Images: 10 (Archivo Iconografico, SA), 84, 133 top (Anthony Asael/Art in All of Us), 118 (Marco Baroncini), 58 (Orlando Barria/EFE/epa), 102 (Jean-Marc Bernard/Realis Agence), 46, 48 bottom, 52, 54, 56 (Bettmann), 34 (Daniel J. Cox), 90 (Aristide Economopoulos/Star Ledger), 79 (Niko Guido), 21 top (Jacques Langevin/Sygma), 83 (Lucas Oleniuk/ZUMA Press), 80 (Gianni Dagli Orti/The Picture Desk Limited), 98 (Tony Savino);
Cursorius Photo & Video Library/Leo JR Boon: 36;
Darren Ell: 32, 77;
Getty Images: 125 (Thony Belizaire/AFP), 51 bottom, 32 top (James P. Blair/National Geographic), 112 (Marco Di Lorio), cover, 6 (Eric Meola), 96, 97, 126 (Dario Mitidieri), 113 (Popperfoto), 121 left (Joe Raedle), 95 (Shaul Schwarz), 114 (Alison Wright/National Geographic);
Global Look Press: 59 (Eliana Aponte/Xinhua/ZUMAPRESS.com), 8 (Imago Stock & People), 26 (Benjamin Rusnak);
Inmagine: 62, 131 top;
Landov, LLC: 81 (Hector Gabino/MCT), 68 (Eduardo Munoz/Reuters);

Lonely Planet Images: 74 (Andrew Marshall & Leanne Walker), 2, 89 bottom (Eric Wheater);
Magnum Photos/Jonas Bendiksen: 18, 99 bottom;
Nel Yomtov: 143;
NEWSCOM: 57 (David J. Healy/ZUMA Press), 23 (Lucas Oleniuk-Toronto Star/t14/ZUMA Press), 91 (Pete Pattisson/ZUMA Press), 29 (r93/ZUMA Press), 35 (Merlin D. Tuttle/Bat Conservation International/Scripps Howard Photo Service);
Panos Pictures: 27 (Jeroen Oerlemans), 100 (Dermot Tatlow), 21 bottom, 123 (Abbie Trayler-Smith);
Photo Researchers, NY/Tom McHugh: 39;
Photolibrary: 63 (Orlando Barria/epa), 25 (Kena Betancur), 13 (Patrick Clinton), 82 (Mark Edwards), 116 (Eye Ubiquitous), 24, 131 bottom (Leah Gordon), 14 (Carl Heibert), 87 (Florian Kopp), 104 (Obert Obert), 94 (Achim Pohl);
Superstock, Inc.: 99 top (Nomad), 70 (Photononstop);
The Granger Collection, New York: 40 (Theodor De Bry), 49 (Baron Antonie-Jean Gros), 44, 55 (Rue des Archives), 42, 53;
The Image Works: 120 (Wesley Bocxe), 117, 121 right (Aristide Economopoulos/The Star-Ledger), 78, 110 bottom, 130 left (Melanie Stetson Freeman/Christian Science Monitor), 109 (Iberfoto), 20 (Larry Mangino), 30 (Sergi Reboredo/V&W), 47 (Roger-Viollet), 110 top (Tony Savino);
USAID/Kendra Helmer: 7 top, 67, 72;
Vermont Center for Ecostudies/Chris Rimmer: 33;
VII Photo Agency LLC/Ron Haviv: 28;
WSPA/IFAW: 38.

Maps by XNR Productions, Inc.